The Club

Monica M. Everett

The Club
by Monica M. Everett

Printed in the United States of America

ISBN 978-1-60477-285-2

Unless otherwise indicated, Bible quotations are taken from the King James Version of the Bible.

www.xulonpress.com

THIS BOOK IS DEDICATED TO:

My dear and precious family:
My husband. whose strength and walk with the Lord was unmov-
able and unshakeable, who carried me, even during our darkest
days. He has been my rock through the years…
And my precious sons, Ricky and Joey, my reasons to breathe…
My reasons to live…

To my sweet and precious baby James
My heart still bleeds for thee…

Acknowledgements

Typical acknowledgements simply thank the people who helped the author write the book. These acknowledgements are for those who helped us to stay alive. I would like to offer my sincere thanks to all those who have helped me and my family since the death of James:

Our Lord and Savior Jesus Christ – it is only because of His love for us that we are able to continue in this journey of life. Thank you for thirteen wonderful years with an exceptional child.

Our parents and family – your loving support has been immeasurable. We are grateful for those who came so far and held us up during those first few days and weeks. Thanks for holding us, serving us, crying with us and singing for us.

The staff at Cannon Cleveland Funeral Home and our friends at Community Bible Church and Community Christian School – without the support, love, prayers and practical help, my family and I would not have made it. Thank you for walking with us step by step during our healing process.

All our friends from Florida Bible Church and Christian School – thank you for the prayers, cards and for the many of you who made the long trip to come to James' funeral.

The Newark, London and Atlanta Continental Airlines staff who went way over and above the call of duty to help us during those first two days and beyond.

Our neighbors in Orleans Place - thanks for demonstrating true Southern hospitality.

Jo Upton and my husband for the dedication, ideas and long hours that helped to take my journals and turn them into a book.

Introduction

To those who understand, no explanation is necessary.
To those who do not, no explanation will suffice.

This book is not for everyone. It is for only a few:

-Those who have loved and lost.
-Those that were born with a love that runs deep and passion that
 cannot be squelched.
-Parents who created beautiful beings, only to have them tragi-
 cally, or savagely, taken by human error, disease, or any other
 way.

The words written in this book are not counsel, but the lamentations of a mother who deeply loved her son. They also describe the
spiritual journey that took place during that dark time.

There is no right or wrong way to grieve and these words are
taken from my personal journals.

If it can bring you any comfort, if it can bring you any hope,
then surely my heart will be glad and the death of my son was not
in vain.

Maybe it will heal a tiny bit of my heart, too.

To everyone reading this book, you are not alone.

There are far too many in this club. Maybe we can help each other; support one another. If you have loved and lost, lament with me, cry with me. I will not tell you to stop.

For only by allowing ourselves to speak, grieve and lament, can we grow.

Then, we can take that next step.

Notice I said 'step.'

It seems one must learn to stand and walk all over again.

But you are not alone.........

There are many with you.

Missing James till the day I die,

Monica Everett

THE CLUB

My tears today are for those of you who have lost a child.

You are now in what I call "The Club":

The club that no one wants to be in.

For the initiation involves the death of your daughter or the death of your son.

You no longer keep up with the pace;

You no longer fit in your regular place.

Your old friends disapprove and your new friends are the broken ones like you.

Have you ever cried yourself to sleep?

Have you ever wept while you were asleep?

Did your body become numb to pain or even to human touch?

Did your soul cry out for help and no one heard?

All these things happened to me.

I have three beautiful boys: the youngest was much like me.

A terrible tragedy took him away.

In the blink of an eye my world was swept away.

I became an alien in this world.

I was no longer in the "Mother's Club."

I no longer connected with my friends whose kids were in the band like mine.

I went from taking children to school -

To never having to go back to school ever again.

My son didn't make it to the eighth grade.

He will not finish high school,

Nor will I hear his wedding bells play.

I feel alone, now.

This book is neither advice nor answers to this life,

But rather an acknowledgement of pain, grief, and despair:

The reality of living life without my child,

The turmoil that one goes through.

The death of a child is cruel and devastating to each and every family member.

I have suffered tremendously due to the loss of our dear son.

I was hesitant to print my thoughts on this matter, but I know those who felt the same.

You are not alone and if you lost a dear and precious boy or girl,

It is with great sadness that I say,

"WELCOME TO THE CLUB."

Preface

It was the evening of July 17th. After a day of practicing soccer, James (our youngest of three boys) and I had just eaten at a friend's mother's house. Ricky, the oldest, was visiting with one of his friends, while Joey, the middle son, was at a youth retreat in Clearwater, Florida. Monica is a flight attendant for Continental Airlines. She was flying over the Atlantic working an overnight flight from Newark, NJ to London. I was going home, and James was going to spend the night at his friend's house.

Then I got the phone call that no parent ever wants to get. James was in a car accident and was hurt badly. As I rushed to the accident scene, my mind wandered with thoughts of just how badly he might really be hurt. I arrived just before the emergency vehicles. James was in the back of the car, slumped on to the seat. I put my hand on his back and said, "James, it's me, dad. I'm here, son." It was at that point that I noticed something terribly wrong – I could not feel him breathing. Then I noticed that there was no heart beat. At that moment, the emergency medical technician showed up and asked me to hold his flashlight while he checked for a pulse. I felt nauseous as he frantically searched for a pulse that he could not find. Our son was gone.

The pain that I experience at the knowledge of his death became compounded when I had to call my sons to let them know that their brother had died. Those phone calls were the hardest calls that I ever had to make. I tried to call my wife, but her flight had already taken off. There was no way to communicate with her until she landed in London. How could I possibly tell my wife over the phone that our baby was gone? I could not.

After they landed, I called the lead flight attendant and told her what had happened. I asked her to put Monica on the next flight out and tell her that there was a family emergency and that I would meet her in Newark. Monica called me moments later to ask me what had happened. I could not tell her. She knew by my tone and my crying that it was bad, but I still kept silent as to what had happened. I simply told her that I would let her know when we met in Newark.

Monica had to be sedated in order for her to make the flight. She had just worked all night, was physically exhausted, and all she knew was that something really bad had happened. I met her as she exited the plane in Newark. She kept screaming, "Just tell me it's not the baby – tell me it's not the baby." The Continental employees escorted us to a room where I had to tell her that it was indeed our baby and that he was gone.

As you read the following pages, you will get a glimpse into Monica's soul. She loves deeply and therefore grieves deeply as well. You will begin to grasp how a grieving mother wonders how she can make it just one more day. As you sense her pain, I pray that eventually you can sense some of the comfort that she has received as well. Our prayer is that you will begin to be comforted even in the midst of the difficulties that you are going through right now.

Brooks Everett

FRAGMENTS OF THE SOUL

What you are about to read are pages from a journal. Some are dated while others are not. Many times I did not know what day it was. Time did not matter to me. My grief was great. There seemed to be no way of escape but to write down my turmoil on paper. Those who have not lost a child, found my process frightening. They were at a loss of what needed to be done, which is perfectly normal, for it is difficult to fathom how intense and deep the soul can bleed.

The wailing and laments of the soul can be very frightening. Like the great oceans of our earth you will notice the waves of my grief and loneliness. There were days when things seemed to turn around, but the next day I would wake up with the reality of the absence of my precious James.

How normal is it for us to awaken every morning and want to go to our child's room to wake them up for school, or just to check up on them to see if they are ok? Therein lies the reality of it all. I still awaken every morning with that desire to jump out of bed and go to my sons' room. But he is not here. I then must fight that urge. Then comes the process in my mind…oh yeah, that nightmare is true. I can escape it for awhile, but I always come back to that empty house. I had to pass by his room. The evenings are the most difficult. I will deal with this till our Lord returns. This is a life sentence.

The difficulties we face in our lives will always be there. The amazing part of this is that I saw the great and mighty hand of the

Lord. He was there in the midst of my pain. He sent heavenly gifts my way and Angels disguised as friends. God is for real and he saw me through those dark and lonely days. I hope the acknowledgement of this brings you comfort. Having someone that has been there seems to ease the burden we carry.

So, come and take this journey with me. If you are in the Club you will understand its language. If you are not in this Club then maybe you will get a deeper understanding of what that person goes through. Maybe you can minister to them, help them. Understand the down times. Understand the depth of that loss. For sometimes all they need is a listening ear and the acknowledgement of their pain. I think of that verse that says it all and the Lord made it so simple for us;

"Rejoice with them that do rejoice, and weep with them that weep."

UPON THE DEATH OF MY SON

THERE CAME A SADNESS WITHIN ME THAT

WILL REMAIN FOR THE REST OF MY LIFE.

Why?

Did God not think I was a fit mother?

Did God think I was so horrible as a parent?

That he had to take James home?

Maybe it was a past sin?

Was it a broken promise?

I know I rededicated my life and promised several things in my
youth to the Lord…

Maybe He was angry with me…

Has it come back to haunt me?

Am I worse than everyone else?

I want to scream WHY!?

WHY!?

On my bed I cry;
My pillow, soaked from tears:

Broken spirit…
Broken soul…
Broken heart…
Broken

No answers
No sense
No justice
No more James.

A MOTHER'S POINT OF VIEW

How many times have we said or heard someone say, "If I lost my child, I would die." Well, I almost did. After I received the news of a POSSIBLE death or horrifying injury to one of my sons while I was in London, I went into complete shock. They called the paramedics, treated me, administered medication, placed me in a wheelchair to put me on an eight hour flight back to New York, where my husband Brooks waited to meet me. I knew it had to be something serious for Brooks to have to meet me halfway. It was there that I learned which one I lost. Up until now, the events that just took place were the easy times.

One of the most difficult things I ever had to do in my life was to walk into a cold morgue and see the body of my beautiful son lying there. It is a miracle that I even survived that. I dropped to my knees and screamed and cried. It was so sudden, just like that, he was gone. I didn't even get to say goodbye. Even if a child dies in illness, there is that preparation. But for me he just vanished. It is a terrible feeling to be left hanging like that. It will be something that will stay with me forever.

Days later I barely existed; I just went through the motions of life... and did my duty for my son. Days passed and I began to fall into great despair, screaming and crying. The reality of his absence was settling in. At one point I felt like I was going to lose my mind because I just wanted to SEE him. I wanted to look at him, be with him, talk to him, but there was nothing; and nowhere to go to find him. As a result of that, I ended up in the hospital days later. When I arrived at the hospital, I barely had a pulse, low blood pressure, shortness of breath and chest pains. They were the symptoms of a heart attack. My heart rate went down to 34. The battle for my life continued all night long and until the next day. At one time, Brooks told me crying, he thought he had lost me. He looked into my eyes and there was nothing there. I could see him screaming but I could not hear him. Through much prayer and me thinking I did not want the boys to suffer another devastating loss, the Lord pulled me through. I always would tell Brooks, the only thing that would ever kill me, is that if something ever happened to James. And you know what? It almost did.

Still, it was not over. I still had breakdowns and could not sleep for more than 2-3 hours at night. Within the weeks to follow I was in and out of the doctors offices for major breakdowns. The Doctors finally gave me medication. One to get me up in the morning, one to make me sleep at night. When you feel like you are going out of your mind, take a Valium. I am still on medication. I go to therapy 2 times a week. There was a time when I could not control my crying and cry to the point where I could not breathe. That is when Brooks would take me to the doctor every 3-4 days to be injected with Demerol or sleep medication so that I can at least sleep for 24 hours and survive one more day. Just one more day. One...day. That went on for weeks. And guess what? I thought I passed that stage, but I didn't. March 3rd, another breakdown, another shot, more medication. This was no way to live.... This was no life. Do you know what triggered it? When my friend had to leave because she had to pick up her daughter from school. I immediately dropped because I.... could not go to the pick up line. Although it was an accident, and not intended in any way, it still amazes me how one mistake could destroy someone's life.

This devastation that has occurred in my life has also physically left me broken. Because of the emotional and physical breakdowns, I had to start all over again. I had no strength. At times I could barely walk!!! It was at least 7 months before I could summon up the courage to drive. My immune system was shot. On top of grief, I fell into all sorts of illnesses. I caught every cold and virus that came around. I could barely get up. Even when I would receive a break from an illness, the grief overwhelmed me. Grief never leaves. As long as James is out of my life, grief will always be present. If I could wake up and brush my teeth without crying.........it was a good day. I would awaken out of my sleep in the mornings sobbing and already fatigued before the day had actually begun.

Everything in my life, of course, changed. I lost my son James, and then the other two because of James. I could not work, which hurt us financially. And in that same period of time, we moved twice. Do you know how disturbing it is to see strangers pack and move your life and family memoirs? It was horrifying.

Unfortunately, shortly after that, Thanksgiving came, and then Christmas. How sad it was to place his stocking on the mantle by his picture. Every holiday in our household was a festive time, now every holiday brings a deep sadness. Every birthday or holiday, even this last Valentines' day was a trip to the grave to pay our respects and place a token of that holiday. Tomorrow we will be going to Cannon Cleveland Funeral Home to attend an Easter Memorial Service for James. I placed Easter Lilies and Daffodils at his grave. How I long for the days that were filled with laughter, coloring eggs and buying a chocolate bunny. There are no more children now. That life no longer exists.

The holidays that I looked forward to in joy and gladness I now face with sadness and dread.

I could not respond to anyone in the beginning because at times I was numb and could not speak. I felt as though I WAS IN A COMA and people were talking all around me. Brooks would read me the cards and letters we would receive and I heard the words, but I could not see nor speak. It is just recently that I have summoned up the courage to finish reading all those sympathy cards. I have yet to read any of those books that people have sent me. Although I am sure they are good books, I have yet to bring myself to reading anything of that sort. At this time, no explanation of this disaster will suffice.

It was the first time in our life that we were not together on James' birthday. The small differences in our life became BIG differences. Joey moved back to South Florida because the memories in Georgia are too painful and Florida had happy memories. Joey is only 17. Ricky stayed in Georgia because the memories comfort him. On James' birthday neither one of the boys would budge. Brooks finds comfort in Georgia, like Ricky and I wanted to run away from this place. Brooks and I agreed that he would celebrate with Ricky here and I would go to Florida to be with Joey. To be honest with you, I did not want my life to be this way. I have only known family. So you can imagine. For me this was devastating. Total devastation.

As for me, this cannot be right and I do not want anyone to tell me that something good will come out of this. When James died, the boys stayed away because they could not deal with it. That crushed me. I still cannot deal with it. It's also put me in an awkward situation when people ask me "how many children do you have?" That question rattles me because I do not know how to answer without an explanation. Not to mention that we have to re-open the wound of telling someone that we lost a child. It will be very difficult if and when I go back to work, where all I meet are strangers. "Do you have any children?" is usually a question strangers ask. Just recently, Joey and I were flying to Ft. Lauderdale and the flight attendant knew me, but was unaware of my situation. I had to explain everything and I could see that it really bothered Joey. The boys, too, have a hard time with having to say over and over, that they lost a brother. Nothing can be good from this...at least for us. Separation of a family can never be good. That can never be right.

How strange life became when there was no reason to wake up and make breakfast, even our BIG Saturday breakfast, or have to decide what to make for dinner, because.....no one was coming to dinner. Nor, to live by the clock: 3 p.m. pick-up, band practice, soccer practice, drama practice, and fall or Christmas programs. I don't have to make cookies anymore or peanut butter and jelly sandwiches, which were James' favorite. Joey no longer asks me to make him brownies. Is it possible for others to understand this? Especially if they still have a full house? If they still have children to look after? I have none. I feel like I've been robbed.

One week before Christmas, Joey announced to us that he was moving out since and I quote: "The whole family thing died when James was killed." (He was living with friends since the time of

James' death). One month later he moved to Florida because that is where he was happy. Ricky now suffers not only the loss of James, but of Joey, too. He misses his brothers terribly. Ricky mentioned to me how people use to call him and say "I just spoke to your brother" and he would reply, which one? He says that now he doesn't have to ask that anymore. Can you imagine that?

As a Mother, at times I cannot breathe, because of the pain and sadness I see in the eyes of my sons. The light has gone out of their eyes. Their perspective changed and they are questioning every-thing. It is hard enough to raise teenagers when things are normal..... imagine when tragedy strikes..........and there are no answers. Their secure and stable environment has been shattered and they don't get it. People tell me that they'll figure it out and come around. But what they don't realize is that yes, maybe, they might. But then it will be to late..... At least for me..........for when they return they will be men. This scenario has robbed me of my last days of motherhood with James, Joey and Ricky. Most men don't see that, but a woman does, because motherhood is everything to us, and it was, especially to me.

Brooks and I are in the house alone and we eventually moved onto the empty nest stage. On July 17, 2004, we lost not one, but all three boys.

Brooks and I have our differences now because he finds comfort in hanging out at school, James' friends, basketball games and youth socials. I, on the other hand, cannot bear to see those things. For me school is out. James was a super star. He was on the basketball team, the goalie for soccer. Played in the band (played 5 instruments over the course of 6 years and excelled in the drums). He stopped playing basketball and joined the pep band and played at all the games. In April of 2004, we traveled to N.C. for a Music Festival and compe-tition. Of course, his band received superior ratings and the judges singled him out as an outstanding musician.

Now for me there is nothing.
There is no 3 p.m. pick-up,
No games to go to,
No band practices,
No plays or drama rehearsals, (which he also was involved
with).
I cannot be around those settings, nor can I be around children.
My children are gone and the life that I knew has ceased to
exist.
I have not moved on (as they say) nor can I go back. I am still in
this dark hole.

I know I jumped off track, but because of these differences my
family has been divided. Not that we do not love each other or care
for one another, but we are all living in a survival state. We all grieve
differently. Unfortunately, it has divided us. People try to give the
pat answers and say, "but you have to be strong and be there for each
other" but every time I would go with Brooks to one of his functions. I would break down and sob uncontrollably. For you see, even
to see a family complete, shatters me, for my family will always be
INCOMPLETE.

I try to see people on a one to one basis without their children
present. I try to steer the conversation away from the events at school
& Church. Do you know how difficult that is? I have experienced
a lot of things and have traveled all over the world, my passions lie
in music, the arts and history and I try to change the conversation
to current events or a different topic. It is difficult to find women
in these circles that do not know what to say if school and church
are not on the agenda. I hope you do not pass any judgment on me
nor that I think highly of myself, I just want you to understand how
strange it is. For those things that I talked about, that was once a
part of my life, have ceased to exist. Besides, it is too painful to be
around that old life. Sadly, I stay home alone while Brooks goes to
his functions. (Alone too, I must add.) Very sad. It's only been 8
months and I have been through so much and so has my family. You

cannot imagine the emotional and physical fatigue I feel at this point as a wife and mother.

I do not know what to say anymore. I hope you understand from a Mother's point of view. What else is there to say? Pray? Maybe, yes, but it does not fill those 3 empty chairs at my dinner table, nor can I kiss them good night.

It is easy for people to move on and think that things are better. But for me they are not better, and probably never will be. All I cared about was my family...and if I can't have that, then life will never be easy or the same for me. I am sorry that my letter has been sad, but I knew, as a mom, you would understand and not tell me things will work out. I finally got up the courage to look at an acquaintances' website....and read how their family was waiting to hear from a Doctor about their child's progress. 20 minutes later, I received a phone call too, but...it was from Camp Memorial...letting me know that James' plaque has now been placed on his crypt. See the difference? They have one thing that I don't have and that is hope. They still have the hope of their child getting better but I don't.

There is a pain that cuts to the core of one's soul and can kill them; that is to lose a child and see the devastation of their family. If you think of these things as harsh, please forgive me, it is just where I am right now. This is what became of my life since July 17, 2004. It is my reality.

SAME NIGHTMARE DIFFERENT DAY

TODAY I WOKE UP IN A COLD SWEAT

I COULDN'T BREATHE

I FELT HEAVY

I CLOSE MY EYES AND THINK

"JUST BREATHE"

THINK MONICA

"BREATHE IN, BREATHE OUT"

"I CAN'T", I TELL MYSELF

I PANIC

"JUST BREATHE", I SAY

I SIGH

THERE, I CAN BREATHE

I LOOK AROUND – IT'S MY BEDROOM

"THANK GOD", I SAY

IT WAS JUST A DREAM

I THEN TRY TO MOVE

I CAN'T

MY BODY FEELS AS THOUGH IT IS TIED DOWN

AT THIS POINT, THE ONLY THINGS I CAN MOVE ARE MY EYES

I LOOK DOWN AND MY BODY LIES LIFELESS ON THE BED

I THINK TO MYSELF, "WHY CAN'T I MOVE?"

AGAIN I CLOSE MY EYES

"THINK MONICA – MOVE"

"MOVE ANYTHING, YOUR ARMS, YOUR LEGS"

I CAN'T

I DON'T FEEL ANYTHING

I TRY NOT TO PANIC

I JUST WAIT

I CALL OUT FOR SOMEONE TO HEAR ME

NO ONE ANSWERS

I TRY TO RECALL WHAT HAS HAPPENED

DID I FALL?

WAS I BADLY INJURED?

NO – IT IS MY GRIEF

"OH NO", I THOUGHT

"IT'S GOING TO BE ONE OF <u>THOSE</u> DAYS"

THE KIND OF DAY THAT WHEN YOU FIRST AWAKEN

YOU KNOW IT IS ALREADY OVER

YESTERDAY I DID GET UP

TODAY I CANNOT

MY BODY HAS SHUT DOWN, AGAIN

I JUST PROBABLY DID TOO MUCH, YESTERDAY

AS I RECALL, IT WAS A VERY PRODUCTIVE DAY

I ROSE OUT OF BED

I MADE COFFEE

I DID A LOAD OF LAUNDRY

YES, THAT WAS TOO MUCH

NOW I MUST PAY

I TRY TO MOVE, AGAIN

I STILL DON'T FEEL ANYTHING

IT'S AS THOUGH SOMEONE GLUED ME TO THE BED

"BREATHE", I SAY

"THINK, IN AND OUT"

AT THIS POINT, ALL I CAN DO

IS BREATHE

I CLOSE MY EYES AND THINK,

"WHAT HAPPENED?"

"JAMES"…HIS NAME EXHALES FROM MY LIPS ALONG
WITH MY BREATH

THAT ONE HURT

IT STARTS TO COME BACK TO ME

HE'S GONE

MY BABY IS GONE

I START TO BREATHE HEAVILY, NOW

THEN I START TO HYPERVENTILATE

I THRUST MY HEAD FROM SIDE TO SIDE SAYING,

"NO, NO IT CANNOT BE"

I BEGIN TO ARGUE WITH MYSELF

"STOP – DON'T LOSE IT"

"JUST BREATHE"

"HE'S OK"

"HE'S IN HEAVEN"

"HE'S NOT SUFFERING"

"AND HE NEVER WILL, AGAIN"

"THINK ABOUT THAT", I TELL MYSELF

I CONTINUE TO REPEAT THAT TO MYSELF

UNTIL I CALM DOWN, AGAIN

"WHEW, THAT WAS CLOSE"

"I CANNOT LOSE IT"

"I CANNOT LET GO"

"FOR I AM ALONE WITH NO ONE TO COMFORT ME"

"JUST LIE STILL AND WAIT"

"WAIT FOR FEELING TO COME BACK TO YOU"

"WAIT FOR STRENGTH"

I WAIT

I HUNGER AND I THIRST

MY BRAIN TELLS ME TO GET UP

I CAN'T

MY BRAIN TELLS ME TO CALL SOMEONE

I CAN'T

I START TO THINK OF NAMES OF FRIENDS WHO SAID
THEY WOULD HELP

I DECIDE THAT I SHOULD CALL, BUT

I CAN'T

I CAN'T REMEMBER THEIR NUMBER

BESIDES, I SHOULDN'T BOTHER THEM

JUST TO BRING ME SOMETHING TO EAT

THAT'S RIDICULOUS

WHAT WILL THEY THINK

I TALK MYSELF OUT OF CALLING ANYONE

I FEEL WEAK, AGAIN

I GIVE UP

I DRIFT IN AND OUT OF SLEEP

THE NIGHTMARES WAKE ME UP

I FALL BACK ASLEEP

OUT OF PURE EXHAUSTION

AND WEAKNESS

I LATER AWAKEN BY THE SOUND OF A CLOSING DOOR

IT IS MY HUSBAND

HE'S HOME

IT MUST BE AROUND 5 0R 6 PM

ANOTHER DAY IS GONE

MY NIGHTMARE IS MY REALITY

SAME NIGHTMARE

DIFFERENT DAY

THE BOW

MY LITTLE BLACK BOW

DID YOU KNOW?

DID I KNOW?

DID I KNOW WHEN I BOUGHT YOU?

YOU WOULD BE THE ONE TO HOLD MY HAIR IN PLACE

AT A FUNERAL

FOR MY SON?

I BOUGHT YOU YEARS AGO

WITHOUT ANY KNOWLEDGE

OF WHAT WAS YET TO BE

LITTLE DID I KNOW

IN 2004

YOU WOULD HOLD BACK THE HAIR

OF A GRIEF STRICKEN MOTHER

AT A FUNERAL

FOR HER SON

Time

As a flight attendant for a major airline,
My life had been ruled by the watch.
Time mattered.
If a flight attendant is 5 minutes late,
She is immediately replaced by one on airport alert.
Airplanes needed to go out on time, regardless.
There is no excuse or error permitted.

I then arrive home;

Boys need to be in school by eight.
Dentist appt. at nine
Grocery shop at noon.
Pick up boys at three.
Soccer practice at four.
Drum lessons at six thirty
Pick up Joey from friends house at seven
Ricky called and he'll be home by eight.
Pick up James from practice at seven thirty.
Have dinner at eight.

JULY 17, 2004 9:25 P.M.

JAMES DIES.......................................

TIME STOPPED

Time didn't matter.

Because everything stopped, along with James.

The day he died, I began to resent time.
Time became my enemy.

I realize its insignificance and unwanted power.
I began to resent its power over me.
I ripped off my watch and threw it to the ground,
As a symbol from me, 'the rebel' against 'time'.
No longer would I look upon its face to consult me
For my next action.

I slept, only when I was tired,
I ate, only when hunger struck.
I depended on loved ones' to inform me of my next step.
'Monica, you have about an hour before the funeral.'
The loving and sympathetic voices of my family
And friends guided me each day.
I became unaware of the light of day
And the darkness of the night.

Up until that point my life was dictated by the watch.
I live now only now to rebel against it.
It's time was up.

February 1, 2006
I pick up my watch out of my drawer,
And reluctantly put it back on my wrist...
I tell myself: only because the planes MUST
Go out on time. It is also a required duty item
As a Flight Attendant.

It is the only time now, I wear a watch.

The Tambourine

It's too quiet.

The drums have been silenced.

My tambourine still placed by your chair.

We used to play, I used to dance.

We'd play CD's and play along.

You made me proud and I made you laugh!

You played so well!! You never missed a beat.

I'd play the tambourine and make a silly dance.

All you could do was flash that beautiful smile,

Shake your head and laugh.

I miss you James.

No longer do I hear that beat,

No longer do I hear that clash,

No longer do I dance.

I can't hear you; I cannot follow your lead.

Where is the music?

My tambourine sits silent,

I dare not move it for fear of that sound,

The lingering jingles of our music,

The ripples of sound,

For if I do, I know I will break.

Truly July 17 was the day our music died.

My First Entry

It was very difficult to put this book together. It was not something to easily digest. It was emotionally painful to re-open those wounds, and feelings. Many times I had to stop and cry. At one point I had to walk away from the whole thing for about 3 days. I couldn't look at it any more. One of the most revealing entries in my journal was the first page I wrote to James. How accurate were my statements and how he grew up to be and to possess the love of so many.

This is part of the first entry in James journal:

April 04, 2000

My dearest James,

I had wanted to do this earlier and I'm finally getting around to doing it. This last trip has been extremely difficult. I have missed you and not a moment goes by that I am not thinking of you. So many times I wish to express my thoughts to you and I cannot. I know some of these things you will not understand until you are older, but every chance I get, I will write of my love for you, experiences from my travels, advice, and lessons I've learned. Most importantly just to let you know how deeply you are loved. You and I have a very special bond...we have been through a lot together.

When you were in my tummy I almost lost you, but by God's grace and great mercy you lived...and you lived to be the most sensitive, caring, godly individual. I cannot express how impressed I was with you since birth. You had a tenderness I have not seen in a long, long time. You are always good to your brothers and I pray that God protects you all of your life. I know you may not understand right now but you have helped me out so much, especially now by your caring spirit. Many times if you saw me sad, you would come over and hug me. You would be the first to come to my aid if I had groceries to carry in or just having trouble. I could never repay you. I have always said you were an angel who fell from heaven. I hope you know that I truly believe that. Sometimes when you ask me for a toy or to buy you something, I have a problem saying no to you! (That's pretty bad since I am the parent.) I feel you deserve so much though and I do not want to deny you anything. I hope you would know by now, I would give you the world. Just please…stay grounded, be grateful for each day, delight yourself in the small things. Make as many friends as you can, live each day as if it is your last. Love deep, and laugh every chance you get. It will be health to your soul. Please keep God in your life daily and the Bible as a foundation for living. It is the absolute truth.

My dearest James, my love for you is so deep and as you know;

You are…
The sun,
The moon
And the stars
To me

Love, mommy

Whenever you miss me, read this again.

HE WAS ONLY 9 YEARS OLD WHEN I WROTE THIS;
NOW CONTINUE TO READ THE NEXT PAGE
4 YEARS LATER….

The Sun, the Moon and the Stars

How odd that day that I came to the conclusion of using the sun,
the moon and the stars to describe the magnitude of my love for
you.
Little did I know when I told you I loved you, you would ask;
"How much mommy?" I would reply, as big as the sun, the moon
and all the stars in the galaxy!
You would just say, "WOW!"

I would then tell the tall tale that I was like the earth. The earth
needed the sun for things to grow the moon as a night light and
keep the tides in place.
The stars? They would be there for beauty and a never-ending
reminder that
There was no end to my love.

Little did I know those three things would be a symbol of your
presence.
I still have your pictures, videos and things but they cannot be
carried just anywhere. So now when I miss you I still see you and
feel you.

During the day when the sun shines I feel you smiling, the sun
kisses
My cheeks and the warmth of the sun calm me.

At night I look for you and see you in the moon, I cannot look
at the moon without thinking of you. And the stars? They are
everywhere!
They remind me of your eyes! They twinkle with delight from just
being alive.
I miss seeing heaven in your eyes. Whenever I miss you I look up,
For those things I see are reminders of you in the sun, the moon
and the stars.

How many times have I told you? Everyday!

At least you knew it. You knew what you meant to me.

July 17, 2004

I spoke to my son for the very last time. We spoke of my trip to
London
And his day playing soccer. When we said goodbye; I said;
"I love you."
He replied "I love you too."
I said "and you are"… (Pause)
He replied; "the sun, the moon and the stars."

His Place of Rest

I could not find it in my heart to bury you.
I could not place you underground.
I could not place my child of light,
In a place
Where I could not see the stars.
I could not place this child of mine,
Where the sun and the moon could not shine.

We did not place you underground;
We placed you in the light.
We placed you in a chapel
Where the sun shines on your place.

The Birthday Letter

This Letter was written on the day of February 20, 2005 for James by Monica.

8:05 A.M.

My Dearest James,

How many times in our lifetime have we recited the words Happy Birthday?

HAPPY//   BIRTH//   DAY.

Yes James, indeed it was a Happy Birthday. It was a precious and miraculous gift from God that transpired to 13 years of insurmountable joy and happiness.

It was upon your death that the depths and significance of those words
Do now hold a new meaning in my life.

I now not think of your birth and the celebration of life today,
But every waking moment.

How we take for granted the power that blows out the candles... that one breath....THE BREATH OF LIFE.

Today will still be a celebration of your birth and the precious life and love you gave to me, your Father, brothers, family and friends.

I will continue to sustain the spirit of your father
who walks in silence and with a heavy heart.
He walks weary still, even in his well doing.

And your brothers?
I will continue to wipe the tears from their eyes.
Their hurting souls I know I now must heal, for they truly and deeply loved you.

I knew all the while how blessed I was.
The bond of brotherhood. It was so tight.
But now that same tight bond has turned to insurmountable pain and sorrow.

LORD, GIVE ME THE WISDOM TO HEAL THE PAIN AND RESTORE THE BROKEN SPIRITS' OF MY SONS.

RESTORE THIS FAMILY. AMEN.

I will continue to lay down my life for your brothers who miss you so much.

****

10:06 A.M.

I cannot sing Happy Birthday today,

I can only weep, because you are not by my side.

Today, I can not lay gifts before you, but only a token of my deep love for you.

Shortly after your death, I learned of a custom in the Victorian Era that when a child died, the mother would take a rose, break it in half
And place it over the coffin.

This was to signify that her heart had been broken.

Today I will place before you the only gift I can,

And that is a token of my broken heart.

James, I hope this will not make you sad,

But show you how much I truly loved and adored you.

****

10:17 a.m.

James, I still can't sing the birthday song, because I have been in deep mourning.

My songs all day have been that of lamentations.

****

11:45 a.m.

We both shared a deep love for music, and I want you to know,
That it has been the power of the music
That has brought me joy in the midst of death and darkness.

****

12:30 p.m.

Well, I just decided. There will be a cake.

The only adornment will be your name. James Michael Everett.

I will summon up the courage to put 14 candles.

Still...I can't sing Happy Birthday. Instead I will play a song by Mozart and

Lay my rose that I broke in two before you.

The lights will be out with only the light of the candles. I will kneel before the cake and try to imagine what you would look like at 14.

I will also remember your love, your laughter and most of all, your smile.
That smile that made every problem I ever had disappear.

After I light the candles, I will play for you Ave Verum Corpus by Wolfgang Amadeus Mozart.

It speaks of Christ's suffering on the cross.

I quote the closing words: May we have tasted of you (indicating His suffering) when we come to the hour of our death.

In this particular moment of time, before our life ends –

Your family has tasted suffering.

****

I also heard a new Opera that was written. It is called, The Transmigration of Souls by John Adams.

It speaks of the journey of ones' spirit migrating to heaven and how those left behind that also experience trans-migration as well.

Those who truly loved them, a part of their soul depart with them.
That couldn't be any truer.

For you have taken a part of me with you.

****

1:45 p.m.

My sweet and precious Baby James,

I have surrounded myself with a few of those who have witnessed your birth.

There is an old saying: When you were born on that day, you were crying and everyone else around you was smiling.

Today it is you who are smiling, and we, who are all crying.

****

2:05

My sweet and precious Baby James,

To our family you were our sunshine.

Your life became as a shining star to those around you.
But now we are in darkness with only a glimpse of the moon.

May the sunlight you brought in our life,
Reflect upon that moon to light a path before us.

JAMES MICHAEL EVERETT

OUR SUNSHINE

FEBRUARY 20, 1991 - JULY 17, 2004

DEEPLY LOVED, CHERISHED AND ADORED

Daffodils

Last spring as James and I set out to run errands we noticed that almost every house had daffodils, even at the entrance of our development. I was delighted at seeing them and would point out each group as we passed them. James would smile. When we got to the main road, jokingly I said, "James do you know what it's it all about today?? It's going to be about purchasing daffodils. Today is all about the daffodils." James laughed since that was a frequent game we played. (Today it's about ... getting to church on time, basketball, the dogs etc).

During our day out we stopped at Wal-Mart, Lowe's, and Home Depot., in search for daffodils to plant. To our dismay they were no where to be found. Through the week we would look, bur never found any. It then became a standing joke between us. He would never let me forget it. He teased me profusely for months. He would say, it's all about the daffodils, huh mom? And I would reply, of course!

Well. The seasons changed and the daffodils were no longer.

July 17, 2004 my precious sweet baby James went to be with the Lord.

February 13, 2005

I walked into Publix today to buy flowers and balloons for Brooks and the boys. But what do I see???? A row of potted daffodils. I felt weak and hunched over the cart. I cried bitterly. I finally found them, but now it was the son I could not find. After pulling myself together I decided to purchase a pot of daffodils to place on the mantel in front of his picture. It was hard to find a good pot since most had already bloomed and the edges had already turned brown. Not one looked healthy. I noticed one that was young with new buds and asked the clerk if they were daffodils, she replied, "Yes, they are newly planted so it will be a few days before they bloom." I was rather disappointed since I wanted to present them to James in full bloom for Valentines Day.

That evening, when I arrived at home, I noticed everyone had already fallen asleep and the silence seemed deafening. The house was also very dark with the exception of the light that hung over his picture. His smiling face, radiant as ever. I set everything I had down and picked up the young daffodils with both hands. With tears streaming down my face, trembling and sobbing, I stumbled through the darkness and approached his picture. It wasn't about the daffodils, James. It was all about you. I fell to my knees by the fireplace and wept uncontrollably.

The next morning I walked downstairs and stopped as I came around the corner. My knees grew weak and I held on to the rail for support. I couldn't believe my eyes. I blinked and looked again and I said, "It can't be." The daffodils that I had purchased stood tall and proud in full bloom. Ironically, there were five flowers. I walked towards the mantel, shaking and thinking that it just couldn't be – it couldn't be. They were too young. It's impossible – or is it that that was my Valentines present from James? Call it what you may, but I think I witnessed a small miracle today. Happy Valentines Day, Mom. Love, James.

Oh, by the way, six months later we moved to our new house. The next February we were surprised to find that over 200 daffodils bloomed on our property.

Your Song

James, remember our song? Our duets?

Remember Your Song by Elton John?

You would ask me to play it over and over;

Of course; I would never mind.

Playing for you was pure joy.

Then one day, you asked me to teach it to you.

Well, I thought; I don't know… it took me almost a year to learn
and perfect it!

But of course, what did I expect?

You learned it in two weeks.

Did it surprise me? No.

You were a brilliant child and I was so proud of you!

I remember the first time I sang and played it for you...

You had that enchanted look on your face,

And your eyes sparkled.

Then, you would give me that shy little smile of yours.

I would sway back and forth and sing

With all the animation and exaggerated expressions I could think
of

And then..........

Lovingly belt out the two sentences I thought..........

Really pertained to you;

That yours are the sweetest eyes I've ever seen.

And

How wonderful life is while you're in this world.

Then I would hug you and tell you,

How true those sentences were for me.

I'd remind you of what you meant in my life.

Looking back at those times James, I'm so glad I did.

I hope you knew the depths of my love for you.

Although it was meant to be a love song,

I would change some words around, so I could sing it to you.

I remember your laughter as I mumbled and jumbled

Some of the words around to make them all fit!

Those words burn in my memory now.

What I would give to see those sweet eyes again.

July 17, 2004

The teacher sits quiet now;

For her pupil now plays for the angels.

James, I have yet to touch our keyboard,

For I cannot bring myself to play it.

It's too painful just to think about it

And it hurts too much.

For now I cannot play by your side.

Oh James, how I miss you!!!!!

At this time,

I feel I can never play again! Not without you!

Not without my precious Baby James.

It's so different now.

How I cried...how I wept...Can't you hear me James?

Strangely enough though, I still hear that song sometimes;

Even without the instruments.

The song;

That song I taught you........ Will always be <u>your song</u> for me.

It plays in my dreams now.

But the words.........those words.....that I sang for you

They still dance in my head.

And somehow the music continues to play.

They picked up a new instrument though:

They now play with my head and my heart,

And sing in unison with my soul,

But this time <u>they</u> changed the words

And they ended it like this;

Remember those two lines that were meant for you? This is how they are written now.....

<u>My sweet child, yours were the sweetest eyes I've ever seen.....</u>

My gift is this song,

And this one's for you.

And I will tell everybody, that this was your song;

It may be quite simple but, now that it's done,

And now, you are gone,

I hope you don't mind, I hope you don't mind

That I put down in words;

HOW WONDERFUL MY LIFE WAS, WHEN YOU...........WERE
IN THIS WORLD.

I miss you, James........Love, Mommy

Seashells

James, we loved the beach, didn't we?

The sun, the sand, the warm waters, all

The sea shells and treasures we would find. (So we thought)!

Best the best thing about it was

All the fish we would see!

I remembered when you tried to catch that

Needle nose fish. You followed it along the shores

For almost an hour! How I miss those long walks

On the beach, talking about life and picking up sea shells.

I still have them James.

Those precious seashells you and I collected.

They are in the jar by my kitchen window,

So I can see them everyday!

Of course, there's that one particular day

I treasure especially, with all of my heart.

This one particular day...............

I could not take my eyes off of you.

You just seemed so beautiful to me.

Your long blonde hair blowing in the wind,

Your face all aglow,

And your beautiful blue eyes that sparkled like the sea.

To me...you peaked. You peaked in beauty.

I thought it was strange, because I thought to myself.

Can he ever be more beautiful than this moment?

Or even, this time...in his entire life?

As we walked along the shore I said;

"James! I'm going to start taking pictures of you

As you walk along the ocean."

Of course, you replied, "WHY MOM?"

I replied, "BECAUSE YOU ARE SO <u>BEAUTIFUL TO ME!</u>"

<u>Of</u> course you said, "Mom, I <u>cannot</u> be beautiful

Because I am a boy!"

I replied, "No my son, It's a different kind of beauty.

It is a beauty that comes from your heart and soul.

That would explain that glow on your face!"

(You made a face)! I continued,

"It's beauty like this OCEAN!"

(I stood back into the ocean and opened up my arms wide).

"Beauty like the Aurora Borealis,

Or the Grand Teton Mountains!"

You just shook his head and smiled. OK.

I began to take pictures as you picked up shells,

Ran in the water and walked alongside the shore.

I took a whole roll of film.

How extreme I thought!

But being 13 and still growing, I knew your features

Would change and I felt compelled to capture this moment.

We walked side by side and passed 2 strangers who asked

Us if we were picking up some pretty shells.

I replied, "Yes! And I have the most beautiful seashell right here!"

(As I put my arms around you.)

Again, you gave me that shy smile of yours.

After walking and talking for a while you said,

"Hey Mom, see those rocks over there?

Let's go sit there and talk! I'll race you there!"

You pretended to run in slow motion for me and

Then took off VERY SLOWLY!! I laughed and replied,

"FUNNY! VERY FUNNY!" You then stopped, (running in place)

Turned your head and flashed that smile of yours and SHOUTED,

"I LOVE YOU MOM!"

Then you took off running!

I couldn't run; I just stood there. I was mesmerized and took a deep breath.

And with all the sincerity in my heart I said,

"I cannot believe how happy that kid makes me.

I LOOK FORWARD TO THE REST OF MY LIFE WITH HIM!"

As I stood there and watched you run to the rocks.

<u>July 17, 2004</u>

James Michael Everett went to be with the Lord.

Those pictures were some of the last

Photographs taken of him.

The song: <u>YOU ARE SO BEAUTIFUL TO ME</u>

Was played at his funeral.

It was the end of May when we strolled along the beach.

There must have been a reason that day

For that glow on his face.

He was getting closer to heaven to meet with his Heavenly Father.

And I was right when said I thought he had peaked in beauty.

I was right.

He had. He peaked.

His life on earth was done.

I miss him now, my little beach buddy.

I walk the beach alone now.

He no longer walks beside me.

The ocean is where I find my comfort now.

At times, I can walk beside it and cry.

I cry out to James and no one can hear me.

The roars of the waves are kind and drown out my cries.

I can go there and cry, for I know he can hear me,

For this is the place where we connected the most.

There is a hole inside of me that will never be filled

And a joy that will never return.

Still, I will never forget that special day on the beach.

That special day when we laughed and talked

And picked up seashells. How peaceful,

How simple that time was. We were so happy

And carefree. Our only worry was finding the

Right seashell.

I will never forget his heavenly face that day,

Nor his laughter...his eyes...his precious smile.

I will always regard that day as one of the

Most BEAUTIFUL days of my life.

Your Shadow

THIS POEM WAS WRITTEN ON AN AIRPLANE ON MY WAY TO FORT LAUDERDALE. MARCH 17, 2005 7:30 A.M.

Why did you sit there little boy?

Don't you know?

Don't you know my pain?

Don't you know my son is gone?

Did you have to have blonde hair?

Did it have to be that long?

I was sitting behind you and had to turn away.

The chest pain, the ache that flushes through my body

Now I can scarcely breathe.

Will I ever be normal?

Will I ever be able to LOOK at a child without feeling that ache?

That painful longing for his presence?

I cannot see your face, little boy,

But from here you look like him.

Yet, I know all to well, you are not him.

For you are but a mere shadow of him.

The long blonde hair,

The same lanky build,

Even your hands....

You must be 12 or 13.

Why did you have to sit there little boy?

Don't you know I can't breathe now?

Why James.....why you?

James. Why did you have to go?

Why did it have to be you?

Will I forever be plagued?

Will I forever be in this pain?

He turns his head sideways now...hmmmm.... wow....he resembles
you.

My body feels that ache that crushes me again.

Just breathe, I say. Just take one more breath.

My body grows weak...If I were standing I surely would have
collapsed.

I must hold on, for I am alone. I cannot breakdown here.

Just breathe. Don't cry. I say. In 2 hours I will be with family. Then I can cry.

He speaks and I have to look up again. Wow.

James, from here he reminds me of you.

But I know he is just a mere shadow of you.

James, how I wish it were JUST YOU!

James, please help me!

Why did he have to resemble you?

Is he but a mere shadow of you for me, so I can catch a glimpse of you?

Is the shadow there just to let me know you're still there for me?

What if the shadow is there to let me know that you...are here with me?

O.K. James, I'll just imagine that it is you sitting in front of that airline seat.

It's still hard you know. Because when we flew, we always sat together.

O.K. James, I'll just close my eyes and pretend the shadow is you.

Oh, my sweet and precious James,

How I wish,

It was...

Just,

You.

I was seated in an aisle seat and he sat right in front and kept
leaning over to his brother across from him.

IRONIC ENOUGH...LOOK AT THE DATE...IT WAS THE 17th...

A Different Kind of Blind

On July 17, my precious son was taken from me.

My life has changed in so many ways.

For now I cannot see.

I was not born blind,

But now I am forced to be blind,

For I cannot see my son.

He was taken from me.

I cannot see a mother with her child…

I have to turn away. I immediately

Receive that blow to the chest,

The shortness of breath, along with the ache

That runs rampant through my body and soul.

This is what happens each time I see

A family who is complete.

They speak of school, they speak of band

And the rushing to and fro.

But it is not that way for me;

For my life has come to a complete halt.

It was then that I was forced to be blind.

I cannot see a playground where children play;

Nor can I go to the park and hear them laugh.

I have to turn my eyes away when I pass the toy aisle,

Or look down when little boys' clothes are around.

I have come to try to avoid children altogether.

I cannot see the school where he went.

I cannot drive over to that side of the building.

I cannot see a movie or television.

For now there are limits.

The rules?

No death scenes, no children, no sentimental family scenarios.

Why? Because now I have no children.

Death has entered my home.

Who let him in?

My two older sons have moved on and out of the house.

They needed to escape the painful blows that death brought in.

They escaped, but I could not.

Death crippled me and scarred me.

The death of my son caused me to choose and accept blindness.

I still can't see.

It also took my dreams of what the future has in store.

I do not know where I am going.

For I cannot see the light.

How and why did this happen to me?

Is anybody out there?

Please help me see!

Lord please help me see!!!

Will my sight ever be restored?

THE UNIFORM

I NEVER KNEW HOW I WOULD FEEL

I NEVER KNEW I'D SEE THIS DAY.

THE DAY SOMEONE WOULD TELL ME

THAT MY BABY BOY HAS DIED.

I SAW IT IN THE CLOSET TODAY,

HANGING THERE ALL ALONE.

THE UNIFORM I WORE THAT DREADFUL DAY.

THE UNIFORM, THE UNIFORM OF DEATH.

HOW MANY TIMES HAVE I FLOWN?

HOW MANY PLACES HAVE I BEEN?

AND YET, I REMEMBER NOTHING.

NOTHING EXCEPT THAT DAY FROM LONDON.

I PUT MY UNIFORM ON JULY 17, 2004.

NOT KNOWING I'D BE WEARING IT FOR THE NEXT 3
DAYS.

I PROUDLY PUT IT ON THAT DAY & MADE MY WAY TO
LONDON.

NO SOONER THAT I GOT THERE & SETTLED INTO THE HOTEL,

I WAS CALLED BACK HOME. THAT DREADED PHONE CALL......

YOU NEED TO GO HOME; THERE'S BEEN AN EMERGENCY SITUATION.

WHAT? IT CANNOT BE!!!!!! IT MUST BE MY DAD.

I JUMPED OUT OF BED, PUT MY UNIFORM BACK ON AND STARTED TO PACK.

IN THAT UNIFORM I MADE THE PHONE CALL HOME...

IT WAS NOT MY FATHER BUT MY SON.

IN THAT UNIFORM I COLLAPSED.

IN THAT UNIFORM I SCREAMED & CRIED.

I FELL FACE DOWN TO GOD & CRIED NOT TO TAKE MY BABY FROM ME.

I KNOW I WENT INTO SHOCK.

I THEN REMEMBERED THE FIREMAN WHO TREATED

ME & SENT ME ON MY WAY.

AN 8 HOUR FLIGHT IT WAS. THE LONGEST FLIGHT OF MY LIFE.

STILL IN THE UNIFORM.

I CRIED & SCREAMED & WAILED TO GOD:

NNNNOOOOO!!!!!!!!!!! NO GOD!! PLEASE!!!!

NOT MY BABY BOY! NOT JAMES!! NOT HIM!!!

NOT MY BABY JAMES!!!

PLEASE LET IT NOT BE SO! BUT IT WAS. IT WAS HIM.

WE ARRIVE IN NEWARK, NJ.

MY HUSBAND IS THERE TO MEET ME.

HE TELLS ME OF THE DETAILS. I GO INTO SHOCK.

ANOTHER FLIGHT,

THIS ONE'S TO ATLANTA. TO SEE MY OTHER BOYS.

WE ARRIVE & I SEE MY BOYS.....

MY PRECIOUS, PRECIOUS BOYS.

HOW COULD GOD ALLOW THIS TO HAPPEN TO US?

IT'S SUPPOSED TO BE RICKY, JOEY, JAMES!! I CRIED!!

IT'S SUPPOSED TO BE RICKY, JOEY, JAMES!!!!!!!

I CRIED & HUGGED THEM.

THEIR TEARS ALONG WITH MINE,

FELL ONTO MY UNIFORM.

WE THEN HAD TO MAKE OUR WAY TO THE HOSPITAL.

WE HAD TO ENTER A MORGUE.

THE DOOR WAS OPENED FOR US & THERE HE WAS,

MY LITTLE BABY BOY, ALONE ON THE BED.

HIS EYES WERE OPENED AND HIS MOUTH WAS
SLIGHTLY OPENED.

I COULD SEE THE BLOOD ON HIS TEETH.

HIS BEAUTIFUL BLONDE HAIR HAD TURNED TO RED.

I FELL TO MY KNEES & SCREAMED!!

THE UNIFORM NOW TOUCHED AND HUGGED

THE LIFELESS BODY OF MY SON.

THE UNIFORM HAS NOW BEEN TAINTED WITH DEATH.

DEATH HAS TOUCHED ME,

DEATH HAS ENTERED MY HOME.

I DON'T KNOW WHAT HAPPENED AFTER THAT.

ALL I NOW IS THAT I AWOKE WITH DEATH

TAUNTING ME.

I LOOKED DOWN TO SEE THAT THE UNIFORM WAS STILL
ON ME.

IT WAS ALL OVER RIGHT THEN, THE FLIGHTS,

THE QUESTIONS AND THEN,

LITTLE DID I KNOW IT....? MY LIFE AS I KNEW IT.

I FINALLY TOOK OFF THE UNIFORM & SWORE

THAT I WOULD

NEVER WEAR IT AGAIN,

OR AT LEAST WHILE I WAS ALIVE.

I DECIDED THEN, THAT I WANTED TO BE BURIED IN
THAT UNIFORM.

FOR IN IT HOLDS THE KEY TO THE TRUE CAUSE OF MY
DEATH.

YOU SEE, THE UNIFORM HOLDS THE TEARS OF A
MOTHER

WHO LOVED AND ADORED HER SON.

THE DRESS ALSO HOLDS THE TEARS OF A LOVING
HUSBAND

WHO CRUMBLED & CRIED ON HER SHOULDER.

IT WAS MORE THAN SHE COULD TAKE.

BUT THE MOST DISTURBING THING THAT THE UNIFORM
HELD,

WERE THE ONE'S SHE COULD NOT BEAR......

AND THOSE ARE THE TEARS OF HER INNOCENT
CHILDREN, RICKY & JOEY,

WHO DO NOT KNOW OF LIFE,

BUT HAVE TASTED DEATH

BEFORE THEIR TIME.

THE UNIFORM ALSO HELD HER INNOCENT PRECIOUS
SON,

THE ONE WHO MADE HER LIFE COMPLETE.

I, MONICA M. EVERETT, WISH TO BE BURIED IN THAT
UNIFORM,

AS A SYMBOL & REMINDER TO ALL:

MY BODY TODAY HAS DIED, MY SOUL TO BE WITH
JESUS.

BUT MY SPIRIT DEPARTED JULY 17, 2004

Taking on the World

I was sitting in the living room, watching the Weather Channel. The entire east coast was smothered with rain. The west coast was the same. The only dry spot was the Mid-West. I sat and thought to myself, "It's an airline nightmare: the delays and then the passengers' complaints and arguments about their inconvenience and discomfort." When I go back to work, will I be ready? Am I ready to hear people threaten me with my job security because they have been inconvenienced? Am I ready to take on the world? How will I respond? How will I be able to listen to them without losing it? I lost my son, and they are a few hours late. What if I break out in tears on the plane with no place to hide? How can I keep up my strength? "Lord, please help me when I again take on the world. Be my guide and my strength."

The Reflection

I had to wash the windows this morning,

For company was due.

I stood on the outside deck and then began to work.

The day was great, I thought!

It was warm and sunny; it even had a balmy breeze.

I began to wipe the windows clean, when

Something triggered my memory;

It was a flashback:

It was you and I, James.

We were in your room spring cleaning.

Then you asked me if I could help you clean your windows.

Our house was on a hill, with a great big drop in back,

So your room was looking out from the top of the 3rd floor!

You asked me for my help to do the windows.

You also asked me, if I could clean them SO well,

We could see our reflection!

Of course, I said yes.

We played CD'S and sang. Laughed about some jokes,

Talked of music and of school till we were almost done.

I was hanging out your window halfway trying to

Clean the outside of it.

You would laugh at just the sight of it.

But you cared about me, because without saying a word,

You held on to my leg. You made sure I didn't fall out!

Shortly after that, we were finished.

Then you said:

O.K. MOM! Let's see if we can see our reflection!

We stood back and there we were,

Standing side by side, two smiling, happy souls.

We were both so happy that we accomplished so much!

Then we hugged. James was so happy to have his room in order.

I thought about that day, as I continued to begin to

Clean the second window. I had to kneel this time since the

Windows went to the floor.

I looked into the glass and

I thought to myself...

If I clean these windows well enough,

Will I see you?

Will I see your reflection?

If I scrub them hard enough,

Will I see you standing next to me?

Of course not, I thought.

But somehow I wish I could.

So I continued to clean and to scrub

And then the glass began to shine.

But wait! I think I see something!

It's a reflection!

It's a face! It has blonde hair!

OH....It's just me, I thought.

It's only MY face in the reflection.

Or is it? Whose is that face in the window?

How sad I thought:

Who is that girl?

That girl in the reflection?

I don't recognize her!

Her face is drawn. She looks tired. She looks so sad.

What's wrong with her?

I can see her eyes from here and I can see her pain.

Even through her eyes, I catch a glimpse of her soul,

And I see how badly she aches.

Tears begin to stream down her face.

She misses someone.

She lost her little boy.

She longs to see her little boy.

She longs to see his face appear in the

Glass just like before...

She longs to see his reflection.

But there is nothing.

Oh James! If only I could go back in time to that moment

When we stood side by side!

Again that surge of pain runs through my body.

I then stood up and wiped the tears from my face,

And realized that I am alone.

I could not see his face.

I could not see his reflection standing by me.

I look again.

I see the girl.

How sad is that reflection with the girl and her tears!

I look at the reflection and see that it's just me.

How sad I say;

that girl in the reflection

she lost her little boy.

Halfway There

Someone took you away from me.

I did not want you to go.

You left so suddenly;

I didn't get to say goodbye, or did I?

Your father said goodbye to you as he held you in his arms.

For he was there, to say those precious words,

As he placed his hand on your heart:

Hey buddy, it's me! It's Dad!

James! It's me, I'm here! I love you James!

But the Lord already had your heart........He had it His hands;

And you heard Him call out your name.............

James Michael Everett.....It's me, your Heavenly Father. I'm here too.

He called out your name!

I didn't want Him to call out your name!

But He did. So you went.

I'm sure it must have been very hard for you to go,

Since you loved them both so much!

It's still a comfort though, to know that

You probably heard your earthly father's voice,

Before you heard your Heavenly Father's voice calling out for you.

I know you did not suffer like us nor did you shed a tear.

Yours eyes were dry and probably twinkled with delight.

Although it was dark then, what you saw was only light.

I'm sure your face was as radiant as the sun.

Your right arm was probably extended to embrace your Heavenly Father,

While you're left arm was being slowly released from the arms of your earthly Father.

I am sure that your beautiful blonde hair was changed,

To threads of the finest silk spun from pure gold.

And your little broken body was made whole again.

I am sure the twinkle in your eye was replaced with

Diamonds and the sparkles from the stars.

What peace to know that you will never, ever suffer again.

But the suffering was here.

At the accident site.

With your Father and Brother

I was not there.

I was in the sky.

It was not meant to be for me to be at the site,

For the Lord knows that I would not be here today

If I had witnessed that scene.

It was not meant for me to be there.

My purpose that day was to meet you halfway.

I stopped and wondered...

Did you stop to say goodbye?

Did you give me an embrace?

Did you kiss my cheek?!

I wonder sometimes....

I like to think that, only because it comforts me.

But because I know you.......

I just imagine that you probably did.

You probably pleaded to the Lord,

To stop halfway,

And say goodbye, to your earthly mother.

Come to think of it,

I am certain that you gave me that embrace and kissed my cheeks,

And then went on your way.

How do I know this?

For when you embraced me, I think you squeezed me a little too hard.

You see, your heavenly embrace weakened me.

As a result of that, I am not that strong anymore.

I am broken and I am not complete.

When the Lord said, "GO!"

I think it must have been hard for you.

Because I think you held me even tighter.

When you left, you forgot to let go right away.

As a result of that.

A part of my soul departed with you.

I am not that strong anymore James, I am now very weak.

For you see, I haven't been the same since you left.

I've been weak and feeling incomplete.

But that's ok James.

It has been all right for me now.

Because I realized what might have happened.

After your heavenly embrace,

I think you accidentally took a part of me with you.

It is a comfort for me to know that a part of me did go with you.

Don't be sad, James

That's exactly how I would have wanted it.

So it's ok James, I will live with this weakness.

I will live with that part of my soul missing,

<u>For I now know where it is.</u>

I am still incomplete, but that's ok James,

Because you were a very special part of me.

It's ok when people say 'she's not the same anymore.'

It is only proof of the impact you had in my life

And the deep, deep love I had for you.

So, it's ok James, that you hold a part of me with you.

WOW!

What comfort though!

That a part of me might still be with you!

Please don't let it go!

Please hold on to me!

Please hold me tight!

I miss you James.

If only you knew.

But somehow I think.......... You do because I am still here.

I am still alive.

I get by, (but barely).

I thank the Lord for the people that have been

Placed in my life and in my path.

I know I have been blessed with the prayers

Of friends and loved ones who have witnessed my suffering.

Please plead to the Lord for a special blessing,

For those who made that dark journey with me,

Who were the beacons of light for me,

And struggled to walk while they carried me.

The dark time in my life that

I had to make that journey through,

THE VALLEY OF THE SHADOW OF DEATH.

In addition to that, what I also know.....is you.

<u>I know you</u> and

I am certain that you kneel everyday,

Before the feet of Jesus

And beg Him to comfort your earthly Mother, Father and Brothers.

I can feel it James.

I can feel you.

At times, of course I wish I were with you,

But I know I must wait......for your Father and Brothers still struggle

And now my life must be for them.

I decided to go back to work sometime in the future,

And continue with Continental. I love to fly. (But you knew that)!

Now that I fly as often as I do to visit friends and relatives,

I think of you and how we met halfway.

For you see, when I fly I see the earth below and many times

I fly way above the clouds.

As I look up, I see perfection; the clear blue sky by day

And the stars and moon at night.

I cannot see you, but I certainly can see the heavens above me.

It gives me pure delight to know that sometimes,

I'm halfway there.

Well, see you later James.

Please continue to beg to the Lord for mercy and healing

For our family.

I know you are truly happy there, but if you get a chance,

And if the Lord would ever allow,

Please put down that precious little lamb you are holding,

And let go of Grandma's hand for just one minute and come.

Please come kiss my cheek.

Give me one more embrace,

But please, please be careful with your embrace,

For I am weak and

Surely this time it might take me with you.

When you see me flying in the sky...

Please come and kiss my cheek...

You know I'll be there,

And besides, I'm already halfway there!

A SAD HABIT TO BREAK

We were driving back from a movie we had just seen together.

Ricky was talking to us about a situation he encountered,

Since the death of James.

He had just finished a conversation with one of his friends.

He closed his phone and said, my friends would always say:

I just spoke with your brother; and I would always have to ask,

WHICH ONE?

I realized I do not have to say that anymore.

For now I know they speak of Joey.

But many times I caught myself about to say;

WHICH ONE?

It hurts to realize I don't have to ask that anymore.

JOEY MOVED AWAY NOW,

AND NO ONE ANY LONGER ASKS.

THE QUESTION OF,

"WHICH ONE?"

NO LONGER EXISTS.

The Last Day of School

Picture a timeline in your mind. Now imagine that it is the timeline of one's life. When does it end? When is the last day? Where in that timeline is the last day of school?

I was coming back from an evening out with a friend when as we approached my door, she says, "by the way, tomorrow is the last day of school." I got angry. My body tightened at the thought and I replied with, "I have managed not to live by the school calendar and you just reminded me of an event that no longer pertains to me." I didn't want to remember; I didn't want to know when that day was, because that day, for me, had already happened.

What, or who, determines the last day? The school? The Principal? The school board? The county? The state? No, God decides. Only God knows when the last day is. The "last day" varies from person to person. Blessed are those who are still in the race of life, those who have the privilege of taking their child to school day in and day out, those who are lucky enough to celebrate the last day of another school year with their child.

I sit alone now and ponder what could have been. School ended for James the day he was killed. School ended for a sixteen year old boy who took his own life in the middle of February. School ended for Linda's girls when they were thirteen and sixteen. Their school bus went into a river – ten students drowned. To this day, Linda can not bear to see a school bus. Oh my, what we take for granted. I just wish she didn't remind me.

"Tomorrow is the last day of school", she said. "No", I thought. Just for some. Just for the lucky ones. That bit of information no longer pertains to me. The last day of school for me was July 17th. You see, school is out for James forever.

I had a very rough day, today. The continuing metamorphosis of my life and soul has left me exhausted. I often ask myself, "Who is this person?" The very actions I once took for granted are now non-existent. What happened to me? From what I learned today – courage had left me. My husband was preaching at two services that morning, so he left the house early. I woke up around 8:00 and prepared myself to go to church. When I arrived at church, I could not bring myself to get out of the car. A feeling of anxiety swept over me like a wave. I was afraid to go in. I wasn't afraid to enter the church, I was afraid of going in alone. I did not want to be alone, but I felt terribly alone. Maybe because the reality set in that I was by myself. There were no children to get ready, no mouths to feed, no shoes to polish, or outfits to pick out. I also missed my husband. Although I know that he is in God's work and doing the right thing, today I just wanted him to be a regular guy. I wanted him to drive me to church, walk in with me, sit with me, and hold my hand. I am not blaming him, but the courage that left me. I tried calling him, but he leaves his cell phone in his desk drawer when he is preaching, so there was no answer. After about twenty minutes of sitting in the car, I summoned enough strength to go in. I felt weak at the knees and sick to my stomach. As I entered the building, I was bombarded immediately by well-wishers. I felt my head spinning with information. It seemed as though they were coming at me from all sides. A wave here, a quick hug there, comments flying by me. I had to look down just to get a sense of my center. Since I was proud that I had finally summoned up enough courage just to come in alone and face the world, everyone's remarks about how hard it was to get there or to get the kids ready seemed painful or trite. I seem to notice more, I guess, all my friends that come to talk to me with their children. They follow their parents around like little ducks. I, on the other hand, looked behind and there was no one following me. In that moment, I wished my husband was there to lean on because I felt I was going to collapse. I take a deep breath. I try to regain my focus on my friends and I see their lips moving, but I cannot hear what they say. All I can see are their children standing beside them. They often notice when I zone out and they ask if I am OK. They ask if I am mad at them or if I feel sick. It is then that I mention James and how much I miss him. At that point, they are not sure what to say since in their mind it has been over two years since his death. I find myself justifying and explaining that I am not accustomed to being alone and that I just survived Thanksgiving. Now I need to find strength for the upcoming holidays: strength for one of the holiest times of the year, Christmas. Oh how I loved Christmas! I remember always praying and asking God to never allow anything unpleasant around that time. I did not want the innocent childhood wonder of that holiday to ever be taken away from me. Now everything has been taken away. Every holiday is tainted with sorrow and grief. I wondered how many people had ever prayed that same prayer. Was I the only one? I doubt it, but my request went unfulfilled. Do I resent God for it? No! I just hurt – I ache. The pain has seeped into my bones. I still struggle with faith issues.

That evening I was speaking with my husband about the events of the day. I explained my experiences and came to another conclusion: I needed a counselor. I needed wisdom and intelligence on that matter. But being at home at 7:00 pm I wasn't about to get some immediate professional advice, or was I? We were into the first week of December and had been moving things around and preparing to set up some of the Christmas decorations. I went upstairs to straighten out my closet and make more room. I opened up several boxes in the closet to find jewelry, pictures and keepsakes. I then came across a box that took my breath away. It was filled with cards and letters from the time of James' death. Sitting on top was a book called <u>Lament for a Son</u>. I liked the title, so I opened it up and skimmed through the book. The words seemed to leap out at me and the agony of his soul comforted me because he spoke of my pain. It was as if I were speaking those words. I felt instant relief. I sensed compassion, acknowledgement and understanding. I started to read the book out loud while Brooks was on the computer. I could not contain my enthusiasm. Although my husband knew my pain, it was healing to hear that there were others who had suffered the same fate. The author spoke with such clarity, intelligence and passion, it impressed me so much. Some of his cries and lamentations were like poetry. I immediately identified with this gentleman as his words expressed the way my soul felt. They were the words that I needed at that moment. They were like a warm blanket on a cold night. I sat and read the book until I fell asleep. I read most of the book that night and I finished it in the morning. It inspired me to continue my writings and to examine my life and actions once more. On with the metamorphosis.

I now realize that God did answer my need for professional help. He did send me a counselor, a wise man that evening. The counselor was found in a box on a shelf. The counselor was author Nicholas Wolterstorff, the Noah Porter Professor of Philosophical Theology at Yale Divinity School. God sent me the counsel that I craved for that evening, my faith was restored.

Psalm 23

It is only now in my life that I feel I have an understanding and a right to speak these words.

"The Lord is my Shepherd, I shall not want."

It is only now that I can truly say I do not want anything but Him. For with the Lord there is life, no pain, no tears, no death. When I see the Lord, I will reunite with my precious son.

"He leadeth me by still waters;"

I went back to these waters, which God created for a purpose.
Waters…a creation of God. My still waters were the ocean;
By those still waters I would meditate and learn to begin to breathe in a new life.

"He restoreth my soul;"

My broken soul, which nothing or anyone could mend. God sent me the power of the music to soothe my aching soul. God used his people to turn my anger into love.
God placed me in a sanctuary to heal.

"My cup runneth over."

My help came from everyone: from family, friends and even strangers.
They came from near and afar. The outpouring of love was a constant flow
The overwhelming support we received made our cup overflow.

"Yea, thou I walk through the valley of the shadow of death,
    I will fear no evil:
For thou art with me, thy rod and thy staff they comfort
    me."

I have been carried through that dark valley,
And now I say with an affirmation in my heart,

"Surely goodness and mercy shall follow me all the days
    of my life and I will dwell in the house of the Lord
    forever."

The Perfect Christmas Tree

We were invited to a friend's house for a White Elephant gift exchange Christmas party. What I thought would turn out to be a normal party, turned out to be something very special. Our friends, Angele and Jeff Dolbier had a surprise for us. When we arrived, they quickly exclaimed, "Don't take your coats off, yet. We want to show you something outside." We proceeded out the back door, onto the yard, following Jeff to a beautiful tree: a tree which they had planted in honor and in memory of James. I was speechless. I just gazed at the tree in amazement. What a tribute. They remembered. They remembered us and our suffering. They remembered James. We all hugged. It was a very special moment.

When we came inside, their youngest son, Christopher, gave me a small gift that was from him and his brother Zach. It was a little ornament: a little drummer boy. I hugged both boys and thanked them. What a blessing that was to me. What a delight those boys were. How sweet to remember. Thank you, family Dolbier for an evening of remembrance.

Silent Night, Holy Night

I had a great moment, today. We were all sitting at the Christmas Eve service singing "Silent Night". I had a vision, and it was my son's face. No, this time it was not James' but Joey's. Of all the precious memories that I have with my three little boys, one stands out above the rest. It was an elementary school Christmas program. Joey's class sang "Silent Night" in English and in German. I remember sitting in the audience being impressed that my son was singing in German. As I gazed over all the children, my eyes caught Joey's. It was as if time stopped. The intent look on his face, his beautiful little round face made him look like one of those Hummel figurines. Joey had silky blonde hair that framed his face. His eyes were fixed upon mine with a gaze that burned a memory in my mind that would last my lifetime. He looked as though he was so proud: he never took his eyes off of me. With our eyes locked, I was smiling so much and I whispered over and over in my head, "I see you, Joey. I hear you, Joey, and I will not take my eyes off of you." I repeated that over and over hoping that somehow he would hear me. I felt as though Joey sang that song to me. Joey and I continued to look into each others eyes until the end of the song when he flashed me that million dollar smile. We shared a memory that will be with me forever and be a light to me on many a dark night.

Now at this Christmas Eve service, I was sitting next to Joey. We started to sing "Silent Night". I cannot hear that song without thinking of that night with Joey. At that moment, the memory of his elementary program became so clear, that Joey's little face appeared and he was singing with his class in German. His eyes were still burning a hole into mine. The vision of the memory faded and reality began to become clear again. I looked over at my grown son and gave him a big hug and kiss. I reminded him of that night and I started to cry. He, still being so precious, hugged me back. I was so happy. I had him next to me on one side and Ricky on the other side, and James in my heart. It felt as though the tears on my face came from heaven – they were James' tears of joy flowing down. For that moment in time I was with my three little boys again.

Christmas Day

DECEMBER 25, 2006

1:30 A.M.

We spent a beautiful day together.

Of course,

Only because we were...TOGETHER.

The Christmas Bible

We have some friends who came over today named Rick and Becky Olson. They have one daughter, Kaleigh, who was in the band with James. It is Christmas day and they dropped by say, "hello" and to give us gifts. What I did not know was the impact of the gift that was going to be given that day. We had sat around the family room and chatted awhile when they asked us to open this one special gift, and what a gift, indeed. They mentioned that this year they wanted to give us something that would go with our house. They had decided on an antique item and they had searched for several months. They wanted something significant for Brooks that would represent him. They decided on a family bible. It was a beautiful Bible that belonged to the Levi Darling family. They had purchased their bible in 1840s. Brooks and I sat, thumbing through the pages noticing old letters, records and events that were so fascinating. They even knew Mark Twain. It was a step back in history, another dimension, and pure entertainment to find newspaper clippings from the 19th century. What an exquisite gift.

I sat there with the bible, thumbing through the pages with restless persistence, skimming and reading the material like a parched soul. At this point, everyone else had already gone back to chatter and games. I then let out a cry that startled everyone else in the house. Of course, my cry stopped everything and they all looked at me. I began to read out loud a newspaper clipping: "Written on the anniversary of the death of James"

"One year ago today"
"And crape was on the door"
"While low, our loved one lay;"
"To waken, nevermore."

"One weary, weary year"
"Of naught but pain and tears."
"O Father, must we bear the weight"
"Of many weary years."

"He was our pride and stay"
"But gone in manhood's bloom."
"We had not thought that such a day"
"Could come to us so soon."

"We saw his precious life go out"
"Go out to meet its God."
"And yet, we could not kiss the hand"
"That held the chastening rod."

"Help us, O Lord to bear the pain"
"At length to kiss the rod"
"And whisper still, while life remains,"
"Thy will be done, O God."

There was silence in the room, no one said a word. The article bears his name and the date of death. To all of us, it was obvious, that they too lost a child named James right before he entered manhood. What a coincidence: or is it? Out of the pages of history, James spoke. Out of the pages of history, God spoke to me once again.

WRITTEN IN STONE

THE BEACH IS SO LONELY NOW

MY SISTER PLAYS WITH HER TWO CHILDREN IN THE WATER

I SIT ALONE ON THE CHAIR

IT'S NOT FAIR

IT'S NOT FAIR THAT THE ONLY ONE WHO ENJOYED THE BEACH LIKE I,

IS GONE

LIFE SEEMS EMPTY NOW

I MISS YOU JAMES

I MISS YOUR PRESENCE ON THE BEACH

I MISS YOUR SMILE

I MISS THE WAY YOUR LONG BLONDE HAIR

WOULD FLY WITH THE OCEAN BREEZE

I MISS PICKING UP SHELLS WITH YOU AND PUTTING THEM IN A JAR

I DIDN'T HAVE A DESIRE TO PICK UP ANY TODAY

I DON'T TAKE MY USUAL WALKS

OH, I STARTED TO BUT AFTER ABOUT 10 OR 12

STEPS I WOULD TURN AROUND AND HEAD BACK

I FELT THE LONLINESS

IT WAS SO STRONG AND IT FLOWED THROUGH MY BODY

AND CRASHED LIKE THE WAVES OF THE OCEAN

IT FRIGHTENED ME

SO I WENT BACK TO SIT ON MY CHAIR

I REFUSED TO GO DOWN THAT PATH AND FEEL THE LONELY

I REFUSED TO ALLOW MYSELF TO FEEL THE EMPTINESS

I JUST STARED AT THE OCEAN AND KEPT MISSING YOU

I MISS YOU MOST ON THE BEACH, THOUGH

I DID NOT FEEL YOU TODAY

I DID NOT FEEL YOUR PRESENCE ON THE BEACH

THAT FRIGHTENED ME

MY SISTER INTRODUCED ME TO A NEW SONG TODAY

I AM NOT THAT FOND OF COUNTRY MUSIC

BUT THE WORDS OF THIS SONG

WERE THE CRIES OF MY HEART

"YOU DON'T KNOW ABOUT LONELY"

"TILL YOU FACE LIFE ALONE"

"YOU DON'T KNOW ABOUT SADNESS"

"OR HOW LONG NIGHTS COULD BE"

"YOU DON'T KNOW ABOUT LONELY"

"TILL IT'S WRITTEN IN STONE"

YOU

DON'T

KNOW

ABOUT

LONELY

TILL

IT'S

WRITTEN

IN

STONE

A Spark Rekindled

In the 1940's, they were high school sweethearts. They went to barnyard dances where they shared their first kiss. Sixty years later, they kiss again, as husband and wife.

My husband, Brooks, was asked by his Aunt Beth to perform the ceremony in Turlock, California. Aunt Beth is a lovely lady who experienced a beautiful life. She was loved and adored by her first husband, Hank, and had two beautiful daughters. As is life, Hank passed away. Ten years later, Beth is reunited with her high school sweetheart, a widower himself, and they get married.

The ceremony was simple, yet elegant. Since all the other guests were immediate family members, I felt privileged to be there. It was probably one of the most sincere weddings that I have ever been to. Everyone could feel the love. They were both in their late 70's and yet they beamed with a youthful glow. They have already been through life, love and heartaches: through children, joy, sadness, new life and even death. So when they stood before Brooks and the Lord, their vows were spoken with truth and sincerity. They had written their own vows that were repeated during the ceremony. He, being a disciplined naval officer, memorized his vows. With all the love and sincerity of his heart, he shared how he would love her, protect her, and provide her with great comfort and his undying love. You could hear the tears flow in that room.

When she spoke, she returned her life and love back to him. What struck me the most was the depth of their passion that was evident from the tone of their voices. These were not young adults, nor children in "puppy love". They were mature, wise individuals who have tasted life, love, suffering and death. They knew the meanings of honor, provide, and comfort. They spoke these vows with a deep confirmation spun from love.

I was enlightened by the weekend and enchanted by their love. It made me believe again, like a little girl, in fairy tales and that true love exists, regardless of age. I was grateful. I was grateful for the feeling of enlightenment, enchantment and the rekindling of the little girl in me, once again. I was scared that the death of my son had crushed her and any good feelings about life, itself. But today, the little girl in me was re-lit like the single candle in the midst of the beautiful centerpiece at our table. Thank you, Aunt Beth, for the spark and for showing me the magic of life once again.

The Homecoming

On the news today, the media was buzzing with the announcement that two little boys who were kidnapped months ago were found again. One was missing for four years, the other four days. They showed the reunion of the families at the press conference. I watched and lived vicariously through them. The homecoming. To be reunited with my son. I watched the parents, scarred from suffering, smile and cry with unceasing joy. The father gave a tearful and strong charge to family and neighbors about the importance of community involvement, neighbor helping neighbor and never giving up hope.

That's when I froze. He went on to say how he never gave up hope and followed every lead. It was hope that kept him alive and that gave him the strength to endure. Hope got him out of bed every morning. I thought about our situation. I did not have to wonder or look for James. I know where his body lies and I know where his spirit is.

My hope lies in the Lord. My hope is the reunion in heaven. Yes, I will hold on to that hope. My husband wonders why I'm glued to the television with these reunions. It is the joy I see in the parents faces. I watched as the mother touched her son's hair and he placed his head on her shoulder. I wanted that. I imagined how I would feel if that were James. What if someone shouted, "We found him! It was all a dream!"? I would hug him and never let him out of my sight! I would kiss his cheeks over and over again!

But what about hope??? Yes I mentioned it before, he is in heaven and I will see him, but what I want to know is: I have a lifetime here on earth; how do I get through that? How do I live without him by my side? How do I exist knowing that the worst tragedy on earth a parent can face happened to us?

I don't know.

THE SANCTUARY

I ASKED THE LORD FOR A SANCTUARY
I ASKED THE LORD FOR A HIDEAWAY
I ASKED HIM FOR PEACE
I ASKED HIM FOR A PLACE OF REFUGE

I NEEDED A PLACE TO CRY
A PLACE TO CALL OUT HIS NAME WHERE NO ONE WILL
HEAR
A PLACE WHERE I CAN SCREAM AND TALK TO GOD
AND NO ONE CAN HEAR EXCEPT FOR HIM

I HOPE TO WALK THROUGH THE GARDENS
AND TALK TO JAMES, I PRAY HE WALKS BESIDE ME
I WANT TO THINK HE WALKS BESIDE ME
I WANT TO THINK HE SEES HOW MUCH
I CRY BECAUSE I MISS HIM

PLEASE COME JAMES, PLEASE COME AND
WALK THROUGH THE GARDENS WITH ME
DO NOT LET ME WALK ALONE
FOR I MISS YOU SO

I WALK
I HEAR AND SEE NOTHING
OR IS THERE SOMETHING THERE?
MAYBE HE IS HERE
BECAUSE THE LORD SENDS ME REMINDERS
OF HIS SWEET & GENTLE SPIRIT
THE SUNLIGHT OF HIS SMILE
THE SWEET FRAGANCE OF HIS GENTLE SPIRIT
LIKE THAT OF A BEAUTIFUL FLOWER
COULD IT ALSO BE BY THE BEAUTIFUL BUTTERFLIES
THAT FLY ALL AROUND ME?
YES LORD, YOU'VE ANSWERED MY PRAYER

YOU GAVE ME MY REFUGE, MY HIDEAWAY, MY
SANCTUARY
A PLACE OF PEACE AND TRANQUILITY.

BLESSED BE THE NAME OF THE LORD.

THE SECRET PLACE

THE GARDEN IS WHERE I GO

WHEN I NEED TO BE ALONE

A PLACE OF BEAUTY

A PLACE FOR PEACE

IT IS A PLACE TO TALK TO GOD

AND CRY OUT FOR MY SON.

NUMB

I HAVE A FOUR DAY TRIP AHEAD OF ME THAT WILL BE DIFFICULT.

I FEEL NOTHING.

I'M TREATED POORLY,

I FEEL NOTHING.

I'VE JUST BEEN HAD.

I FEEL NOTHING.

I JUST LOST $200.00 SOMEWHERE IN THE AIRPORT.

I FEEL NOTHING.

I JUST SHOWED UP TO WORK ON A DAY OFF.

I FEEL NOTHING.

I SEE A FAMILY SITTING TOGETHER ON THE PLANE,

I FEEL PAIN.

IT'S THE ONLY THING I FEEL.

APATHY

ASK ME IF I CARE??

ASK ME IF I AM CONCERNED??

THAT'S THE PROBLEM YOU SEE,

I DON'T CARE!!

I HAVE LITTLE TO HOLD ONTO,

AND IT SEEMS LIKE,

FEWER REASONS TO LIVE.

"JUST ONE MORE DAY", I SAY!

BUT THE REASONS ARE DWINDLING.

THE SCALES ARE BEING TIPPED...

TIPPED TO THE OTHER SIDE.

WILL YOU GIVE ME ONE MORE REASON??

WILL YOU GIVE ME JUST A LITTLE HOPE?

BECAUSE I CAN'T SEE TOMORROW.

A Mother's Sorrow and Prayer

My sweet and precious baby James, how I miss you.

Can anyone bear such pain?

Can anyone bear such sorrow?

"Not I", I said.

For it is too much!

My heart does hurt and my bones do ache

An unimaginable pain

I am so weak, so tired, so broken.

Help me Lord, please Lord.

Help me make it through another day.

Greek Mythology

Whenever relatives come to visit I delight in taking them around town to museums and historical sites. This particular trip we went to Oakland cemetery, Atlanta's oldest cemetery. We came upon a statue that made me stop in my tracks. It was a woman bent on one knee and she appeared to be devastated. Wow, I thought, that looks like me. That is how I always feel. The guide went on to tell this story;

In Greek mythology, this lady had 13 children.
She loved them more than anything in this world.
The gods were jealous because her love for her children
Far surpassed her love for them.
The gods became angry and took away her children.
She wept bitterly day and night.
After a long while, the gods became weary of her cries.
Day and night she cried to them for their return.
But the gods became weary of her and turned her to stone.
So they wouldn't have to hear her cries anymore.

Long after the guide left I just stood there, mesmerized by this statue, thinking how it was the perfect picture of me. Although I was standing there, my soul, like that statue was always crying and on bended knee.

DID HE KNOW?

JAMES,

DID YOU KNOW HOW MUCH I LOVED YOU?

DID YOU KNOW HOW MUCH I CARED?

CAN I SLEEP AT NIGHT KNOWING YOU MAY HAVE
SUFFERED??

HOW CAN THIS HAPPEN?

HOW COULD THIS HAVE HAPPENED?

I FEEL AS THOUGH I'M DEAD INSIDE.

YOU BOYS WERE THE ONE THING THAT MATTERED IN
MY LIFE,

THE ONE THING THAT KEPT ME GOING.

AND NOW ONE OF YOU IS GONE.

MY ONLY REWARD IN THIS LIFE.

WHO COULD SURVIVE?

WHO COULD MOVE FORWARD?

WHO WOULD EVEN WANT TO?

FROM THIS POINT ON LIFE WILL BE JUST WORK.

WORK WITHOUT THE WEEKEND,

WORK WITHOUT EVER GETTING A CHECK.

THE JOY IS GONE.

THE REWARDS ARE GONE.

THE FAIRYTALE IS OVER.

JAMES, DID YOU KNOW HOW MUCH I LOVED YOU??

DID YOU KNOW HOW MUCH I CARED??

GARDEN DEDICATION

I dedicate this garden to
Those who did not survive
For those who cried and
NO ONE HEARD

To those who loved and lost
To those who were left with
Just the broken pieces

To the Mother's who sat in darkness
Afraid and all alone
Who had to avoid the joys and festivities of life
And were left behind to mourn
For those Mothers who could not bear
That first day of school

To the Fathers who stayed strong
And grieved in silence, until illness took its toll

To the siblings who lost their special playmate
Their brother, their sister, their best friend
To family members whose heart and spirit
Were broken forever
I will work and toil to keep their memory alive

But the heart of my garden dedication goes out to

THE MOTHER

WHO IS
THE SILENT STRENGTH AND BEAUTY
OF HER FAMILY'S LIFE

She was left without tending nor care, but now
Rejoices by the side of her child
For now she truly has peace

REST IN PEACE

I look after this garden

To show I care

To remind everyone I know

To love and to care

EMBRACE THE BROKEN MOTHER!

EMBRACE THE BROKEN FATHER!

HOLD FAST TO THEIR CHILDREN!

DON'T LET THEM SLIP AWAY!

NURTURE THEM, LISTEN TO THEM, AND LOVE THEM
UNCONDITIONALLY

CARE

BEAUTY AND PEACE WILL I UPHOLD

IN MEMORY OF THOSE WHO DID NOT SURVIVE

THIS IS WRITTEN IN MEMORIAL

FOR ALL THE MOTHERS WHO DID NOT SURVIVE

AND TO THOSE WHO WALK THIS EARTH

WITH BROKEN SPIRITS AND HEARTS

The Tortured Soul

Once again, I awaken with my tortured soul. Not even sleep has its escape. I often think and count the minutes when a day would end. Always hoping, always praying, that maybe if I just get some sleep I would feel better. But it is never the case. Every night I contemplate whether or not to take a sleeping aid. I battle this because most of the times that I do fall asleep (and rather quickly), I suffer nightmares.

Ever looking, ever searching.
Always looking for James.
Every scenario seems to be the same, except the location.
One involves a house with many rooms. A neighbor states she saw someone take James inside. The entire family runs in and starts to open every door but he is nowhere to be found............

A family picnic at the park that starts out wonderful until someone runs up to me and says that James is missing.........

From the start, I've had this dream every night for weeks;

We are at a lake where all the children are swimming and the parents on shore socializing. The lake begins to churn and some kind of force starts causing them to drown. All the parents run in to save their children. All the parents manage to pull their children out, except me. I am left, wading in the water, calling and looking for James.

I finally stumble onto a body in just about two feet of water. It's too late. The water has stopped churning and is clear, but it does not matter. It's James and he is lying at the bottom with his hair flowing. His eyes are open and he is gone. All were saved but him. I look up and all the children are crying with parents trying to comfort them. I.......just carry mine out of the water and place him on the sand and cry. I look around. Again, to see that yes, it's true ....all were saved, mine was the only one that drowned.

Tonight I had a dream that he was a baby and someone snatched him out of my arms and took off. The desperation of that moment woke me up. It is 4:50 a.m. Of course these are just a few examples of my nightmares.

Is there no end to this tortured soul?
Is it not enough that I have lost?
Is it not enough that I have been robbed of joy, sleep or peace?
Surely, is not enough that I cannot see his face nor touch his hair?

It is strange how deep the toll of death brings upon one person. It affects their health, their wealth and their mental stability.

It is not that my mind wallows in guilt, but being human, we all carry some baggage.
It is the desperation of a soul lost. Where is he now? Heaven of course. Naturally though, I want to see him. I want to talk to him.

Where is the child with the starry eyes? The one who lit up the room simply by entering it! My little buddy!

I cannot keep up with the pace of others. I cannot run with the crowds. My body is broken and the pain runs through to my bones. My mind is in torment over the loss and brokenness of our family. The damage and hurt done to our sons is almost unforgivable.

Why James? Why did the Lord take you?

The Presence of God

Well, I made it through another day. I finally conjured up enough strength to make myself some tea and sit outside. I talked myself into thinking that if I could just make it outside, I would be fine. Rarely am I ever right, but this time I knew it to be true!

I put together my tea tray with sugar, milk, and a hummingbird teapot that my sister gave me. It was a gentle reminder of her love. I have little gold spoons to stir the tea and a delightful little teacup given to me by my Auntie Dorothy. The outside of the teacup is a royal blue lined with 24 caret gold. A picture of a neighboring English countryside is painted on the inside. Such lovely details! One cannot be sad at such a sight!

As I looked around I felt like I could catch yet another breath. "Good", I said, "Just one more breath". I could then breathe a little deeper. The beauty of the property was overwhelming. The air was crisp and clean. The butterflies were still fluttering about from flower to flower. The gentle breeze was blowing the colorful leaves safely to the ground. The sky was so blue, it was majestic and proud! It took my breath away. Being October, need I mention the colors of the Fall? The brilliant yellows, the bright reds and the deep fiery orange that could even make the reds very jealous! As I sipped my tea and took in the wonderful sights, I realized that God was still there for me.

The last 48 hours were a blur. I slept and could not muster up the energy to get up. I was very sad, again, because for me, it was another long night. Joey had gone back to South Florida and again, I missed my family being whole. I missed James and Joey, again. I missed the five of us being together. I would still be picking up and dropping off at school, making family meals in the evening. Helping with homework, and driving them to games, birthday parties, and friends' houses.

But the house got quiet once again: an eerie reminder of the impact of the death of James. The voices of the children have been silenced. There is no one to pick up or drop off. Their friends no longer call or come over. My husband and I will never, ever see that chapter of their lives again.

Those chapters in our family history could not be written. The book will always have a gap. There will always be missing pages. This change that took place overnight would make even the strongest of strong crumble or collapse.

I wonder sometimes if it is not God who put me to sleep. He allows me to sleep when the pain becomes unbearable. Something strange came over me the last 48 hours and I could barely keep my eyes open. I couldn't understand it, but maybe now I do. Maybe he put me to sleep so that this cup of sorrow would pass me by once again.

Coming out of that sleep I awakened with new strength. I went outside and He was there – God was there. I cannot explain how, but I had this gut feeling that I was not alone. It was too beautiful and my spirits were lifted immediately. I felt such a strong presence that I looked around to see if anyone was really there, but there was no one. I listened in the stillness and I knew. He was there. He was there to meet me with all the beauty and glory of His earthly gifts.

For quite some time I felt He had abandoned me, but this time I felt He was there to meet me as I stepped outside. Not that He was really standing there, but I did feel His presence. So many times I have heard that phrase, but not since the death of James had I really felt it or known it to be true. He was there from me when my night (that lasted 48 hours) was through. He was there to show me all that was beautiful still.

As I sat in the garden, there were the sights: the trees, the flowers, the butterflies. There were the songs and the melodies of the birds that sang His praise. Somehow I felt that He was there to greet me.

So, I walked around the gardens and it seemed that He walked beside me and pointed out the beauty. I stared at the beauty in awe.

I went back and sat for awhile with another cup of tea and took in more of God's beautiful creations. The beauty of the day told me He was still there. I felt like I was awakened out of a deep, deep sleep.

~~~~~~

THE STORM CAME IN AND THE SEAS WERE ROUGH,

BUT THE LORD PLACED ME SAFELY ON HIS BOAT

AND I SLEPT. HE WAS AT THE HELM AND

BROUGHT ME SAFELY TO THE SHORE.

~~~~~~

MY NIGHT SEEMED LIKE A LONG ONE. BUT THEN AGAIN HE REMINDED ME, THAT HE WAS THERE AND HE CARRIED ME THROUGH THE NIGHT ONCE MORE. AND NEVER WILL I FORGET: THAT JOY COMES IN THE MORNING.

Do you believe in miracles?

The minute I finished writing this letter, the sun appeared through the trees where I sat. As I finished the last sentence, I saw the shadows move and the sunlight creep up over my page and onto my face. I looked up and the sun was blinding. All I could do was close my eyes and let the warmth of the sun engulf me. The warmth surrounded me and I indulged in it and I thanked God for that moment. "Coincidence", you say? Not for me. I felt embraced by the Son and by my own son.

I would like to thank the angel who watched over me those 48 hours. In my drifts, I saw his face, my husband. He coddled me, fed me, and brought me lots of water to drink: he prayed with me. I thank God for my loving husband.

Sensitivity

A friend of mine called me and asked how I was doing. Unfortunately for her, I was not doing well this day. All last week, I felt weak and tired. I cried everyday. Everyday, something triggered a memory and I would break down. The crying left me exhausted and not functioning.

She seemed a little confused and asked how my crying was compared to the previous year. I replied, "What? What do you mean, 'Last year'"? "Well", she said, "Is it less? Is it better?" I struggled to answer her question and then we hung up. After that conversation I was left feeling cold and unsure.

What is it, people? Do you not know what happened?
I did not lose a job.
I did not lose a house.
I lost a life: a child.

Flesh of my flesh, bone of my bone, I lost my baby.

The answer is NO!

No, it will not go away. No, it does not get better.

I lost a child
Do you not know the value?
Do you not know the cost?
Think about this:
What was the one thing that God gave to prove His love? The life of His Son.
What was the one thing that He knew would show the ultimate sacrifice? The death of His Son.
What would be the one thing that would hurt Him the most? Separation from His Son.

I lost one of the greatest gifts that God has ever given me. I had to succumb to the greatest sacrifice. I am dealing with what is the greatest and most painful loss imaginable. I lost my precious son.

I do not take this lightly, and neither should anyone else. So my cries will always be there. My sorrow will always be there: this year and the next. For it will be years before I will see his face again, and years before I can, again hear his voice. It will only be upon my death that my pain will finally heal. Then, folks, I will be able to move on. For then I will be complete; I will be whole. But for now, his birthdays will be silent and when I call him he doesn't come.

The tragedy of this affair is that it is a life sentence, except this time at a much slower pace. Everyone has passed me by. When they speak of their son's or daughter's graduation, I mourn over my son's graduation that will never take place. When they speak of college, I mourn because James will never be in college and I sit and wonder about what could have been. Life keeps moving for them, but I am standing still. When they speak of marriage, I mourn, for I will never see him walk down the aisle. They proceed forward, I stand alone, still. When they speak of grandchildren, my heart breaks, for I know that I will be kept from God's future gifts to me through James.

His genes, his face, his heart, his spirit and talents will never be duplicated, nor matched. He was a carefully crafted, intelligent creation of God. That is what I lost.

Sensitivity 2

Acknowledge the greatness of the loss. What was lost was a life, a living soul: something that can never be replaced.

Do not discredit the loss as if it were an item. Many confuse this loss with those that fit into the "be strong, keep moving, get on with your life" category. But this was not a thing; it was a soul, a precious, breathing soul.

Have we lost the luster of life? Have we become apathetic towards a human life? Remember sensitivity – a lost art in our culture. We, as a nation, and society, have seemed to have lost sensitivity.

How many times have we heard, "Listen before you speak.", "Choose your words carefully."? I have had to learn these, as well. We all love to brag or boast, myself included, about our families, lives, work or hobbies and accomplishments. But would you brag about your marathon or complain about your painful knee to a soul in a wheelchair? "Absolutely not!" you say. Of course – that is the obvious; but what about the not so obvious?

The woman who bore no children: can you spot that one?

The person abused as a child?

The one who just buried a loved one?

Of course you can't, unless you listen first. You won't know unless you get to clue into them first, before you speak. Then, you may gain some insight. Before you brag about your children, consider if there was a loss or a tragedy.

I remember sitting in a "Grief Care" meeting explaining how simply going into a store and seeing something that made me think of James caused me to feel pain in my chest and shortness of breath. Believe it or not, it was a simple thing: a Spider Man T-shirt. My son James loved Spider Man. I continued shopping, but with tears streaming down my face. After this explanation a friend commented, "That's how I feel about school busses." "Wow!" I thought. What a shame. My memories of my childhood and riding the big yellow school bus are warm and pleasant. These busses haven't changed much in appearance and they are still seen everywhere. But, woe to my friend Linda. She lost two daughters in a school bus accident.

Their youth group went to a camp by a river. The weather took a turn for the worse and the river flooded. As they were leaving the camp, the river flooded and washed the bus into rushing waters. Ten children died that day. The body of one of Linda's daughters was never recovered, the other one washed ashore. The tragic toll that death took on her family also took the life of her husband one year later. She remains with one soul left, her son.

Every time I see a school bus, now, I pray for Linda

Sensitivity, folks! Adapt sensitivity!

A Letter to a Friend

This was written after a four day visit with my dear friends in Moline, Illinois.

My dearest Abby,

I felt compelled to write and now I feel speechless. So much has transpired in four days. I found myself at another turning point in my life journey. I thought about all that we shared and realized I had made another progression. The time I spent with Aaron was special. Instead of thinking of my pain with James, I was able to focus on Aaron. Aaron's needs, Aarons interests. That was a big step for me! For such a long time to look at a 13/14 year old boy was painful. My heart would simply ache. I felt like I couldn't even bring myself to talk or spend time with them. Spending time at your house, I was able to focus on him and not my pain. He was so sweet to me. His gentle spirit was a reminder of James. I noticed I had made an improvement in my journey towards healing. Wow! Little does Aaron know the blessing he has been to this mother's broken heart. I caught glimpses of James all weekend. In his innocent, sweet spirit he patched up a little piece of my broken heart.

"Even a child is known by his doings" Proverbs 20:11

Thank you for receiving me into your home and sharing in your daily life. I enjoyed being a part of the big family, and getting hugs from the boys like I use to when they were little. I love you so much and I will always have a special place for you in my heart. Give Aaron a big hug and kiss for me. You should be proud of him, how he ministered to me. God used him in a big way!!!

Love you!! Monica

LITTLE TREASURES

HOW I MISS YOU BY MY SIDE

SINGING, LAUGHING AND MAKING UP SILLY SONGS

HOW CREATIVE YOU WERE

HOW I ENJOYED THOSE MOMENTS

THEY ARE NOW THE TREASURES OF LIFE

OH, WHAT I WOULD GIVE FOR JUST A GLIMPSE OF YOU

TO SEE YOUR FACE, TO SEE YOUR EYES

TO AGAIN WITNESS YOUR FABULOUS SMILE

I KNOW NOT WHAT ELSE TO GIVE YOU

FOR YOU ALREADY HAVE MY HEART

Joy in the Garden

Basking in the sun

The sound of the woodpecker

The scamper of squirrels

The beauty of the butterflies

The rustle of the leaves

The sweet, sweet smell of the roses

The brilliance in the colors of the flowers

The sound of the old wooden swing rocking in the breeze

The buzzing of bees around the lantana and the butterfly bush

The splashing sound of the birds in their bird bath

The birds' song

The gentle sound of chimes blowing

In the wind

Joy, joy, joy

Joy in the garden

This is my garden.

This is a gift from God.

A sanctuary to rest, to cry and to heal

HURRY SPRING!!!!

O Beautiful little flowers,
Where did you go?

O beautiful little butterflies
Where did you go?

O my sweet little hummingbirds
Where did you fly to?

You went to sleep
You went to spend
The night
Where it is warm.

O my sweet little friends
I will be here
Waiting for you
To see you again in spring.

MY MOTHER'S MEMORIAL

FOR HER PASSION

FOR HER LOVE OF LIFE AND BEAUTY

FOR THE BEAUTY SHE POSSESSED

FOR THE CREATIVITY THAT RAN THROUGH HER VEINS

THIS MEMORIAL IS DEDICATED TO MY MOTHER

MARGARITA DIBBLE MENDEZ

The Absence of Your Smile

My time with you was short.

My love for you had no end.

The sweetness of your laughter would help me through another day.

The silence of your laughter took my breath away.

The sparkle in your eyes let me see heaven.

The absence of your eyes left me in the darkness.

The love in your heart helped me to live.

The knowledge of your love and wishes is what keeps me from death.

The smile on your face turned my night into day.

The disappearance of your smile left me in the dark.

The hugs every day were a source of my strength.

The emptiness I feel takes my strength away.

The kisses you gave me were magical and sweet.

Now all I can have are the kisses of an angel

When I am asleep.

A Small World

I've come to the conclusion that it is the loneliness, the empti-ness of the house that I cannot bear. The silence of this house is deafening. It screams, "They are not here! Your sons are not here!" Everyone goes through this when the last child leaves, but mine left young; mine left before their time. I spoke with a good friend of mine who has two children who are both moving out in January; one to her own apartment and the other to college. I could sense her sadness. She went on to say how she will be like me: in the "empty nest" stage. Another battle she faces is the second guessing and reflections of life: Did we do the right thing? Did we raise them properly? Maybe we should have…all normal questions at this stage of life. I nodded my head in agreement.

During the day, it seems to be different. Maybe because the pattern was the norm; the children would have been in school. It is the afternoon and evening that I found to be difficult. Dinner time rolls around and for a second I panic thinking that I didn't plan anything, but then I remember… no one is coming to dinner. As the evening progresses, it seems to get harder. I look at the time and it is only 6:30 pm. I remember homework. I remember laundry and setting out uniforms for the next day. I remember the hugs. I remember their kisses and I remember their love. How blessed I was to have such loving children. How blessed I was to have such a beautiful family. Now only the memory remains.

I feel myself gravitating towards the sofa and turning on the tele-vision. Oh, I know, I should do something more productive, keep myself busy – all the great advice that people give to me. What they do not realize is that the energy is gone. I am no longer whole. I am no longer complete. A large part of me is missing. So, I lay on the sofa, and watch TV. I begin to flip channels, yet I find it difficult to find anything worth watching. I watch the news, but it saddens me when I see parents hurting their children. I continue channel surfing, and I keep finding shows with whole families – those are out altogether for me. I usually end up watching documentaries and eventually turn it off. Everything else seems to be off limits.

Oh, what a small world I live in now.

PEACE IN THE VALLEY

OK, THAT LEFT ME SPEECHLESS. THANK YOU. WE STILL HURT. THE WORLD HAS MOVED ON WHILE WE STRUGGLE THROUGH ANOTHER DAY. THE VOID HE LEFT WILL ALWAYS BE THERE. NOTHING WILL EVER TAKE HIS PLACE.

LAST NIGHT WHEN I WAS ALONE, THE REALITY SET IN & I FELT PARALYZED. I JUST SAT IN THE CHAIR UNABLE TO MOVE. IT WASN'T TILL ABOUT 12:30 THAT I GATHERED UP THE STRENGTH AND ONLY TO GO TO BED. I MISS BEING A MOM, I MISS JOEY BEING AROUND, I MISS MY MOM, AND I MISS GOING TO SCHOOL & ALL THE ACTIVITIES. THE HOUSE IS SO QUIET.

JAMES WAS STILL AT THE AGE THAT HE LOVED TO DECORATE FOR HALLOWEEN. WE WOULD HAVE SO MUCH FUN. I KNOW THAT THIS COMES TO EVERY ONE'S LIFE, BUT WHEN IT IS TAKEN BEFORE IT'S TIME AND THERE ARE NO OTHER CHILDREN IN THE HOUSE, THAT FEELING OF UNFINISHED BUSINESS EATS AWAY AT YOU, NOT THAT YOU WANT IT TO. IT IS JUST A NATURAL HUMAN INSTINCT TO SEE THINGS THROUGH. I WAS NEVER ABLE TO SEE IT THROUGH, (MIDDLE SCHOOL, HIGH SCHOOL, GRADUATION, AND WEDDING) HOW MANY PARENTS TAKE FOR GRANTED WATCHING WITH THEIR OWN EYES A GRADUATION, A WEDDING, A SOCCER GAME, THE FACE OF THEIR CHILD WALKING UP TO THEM WITH ARMS EXTENDED READY TO HUG THEM? JAMES DIED TOO SOON & JOEY LEFT BEFORE HIS TIME. THIS IS VERY DIFFICULT TO DIGEST AND DEAL WITH. I DON'T THINK I WILL EVER BE ABLE TO SHAKE THAT FEELING OF "UNFINISHED BUSINESS." WE WERE LEFT HANGING: AND WITHOUT ANY ANSWERS OR CLOSURE. I KNOW I SAID TOO MUCH BUT THIS WHAT I AM DEALING WITH, THIS IS MY REALITY.

I HEARD A SONG SUNG BY ELVIS A COUPLE OF WEEKS AGO. IT WAS BEAUTIFUL. HE SANG IT WITH A MEN'S QUARTET: ACCAPELLO. IT WAS, "PEACE IN THE VALLEY". IT TOUCHED ME SO, BECAUSE IT TALKED OF LIFE'S STRUGGLES, BUT THEY WERE NOT GOING AWAY. HE CAME TO THE CONCLUSION THAT WHEN HE DIED & WENT TO HEAVEN IT IS THEN THAT HE WOULD HAVE TRUE PEACE. I KNEW THAT WAS FOR ME. THERE WILL BE NO PEACE ON THIS EARTH, AT LEAST FOR ME TILL I SEE JESUS AND GET TO HUG JAMES ONCE MORE.

BURIED TREASURE

Somewhere in the Atlantic Ocean between the Bahamas and Florida lie two red carnations floating in the ocean.

My sister Debby and I had taken one of those one day excursions to the Bahamas for fun.

I was pretty hesitant at first not knowing how I would feel since the last time I took a cruise, James was alive and we were all together.

Going through each stage of the embarking process I remembered vividly, with every minor detail the excitement we had as a family going away.

For the rest of the week our family enjoyed luxuries such as 24 hour room service, divine meals, island hopping, and excursions that included swimming, petting stingrays, hiking in the rainforest, and cave tubing.

James particularly enjoyed it and asked if we could go on another cruise again.

As a matter of fact, he said "How about once a year?" I replied "yes."

Ten months later, James was gone. That was our first and last cruise. As much as I loved going on another cruise, I thought I could never go again. At least not without James.

Today was a big step for me. I was feeling strong and I wanted my sister to experience the islands, a cruise, and get away.

I agreed to go, but my mind was with James and my heart felt pain. Once I was on board I remembered the good feelings. The smell of the ocean, the bright warm sun beating down on my skin.

The sound of the crashing waves against the ship. I remembered how James and I loved to hang out by the rails and look out over the ocean.

I did that again but this time with confusion in my heart. Happy to see the ocean but sad that he was not standing next to me.

How I missed him and oh how I cherished him.

My sister and I had a marvelous time together chatting, sunbathing on the deck of the ship, shopping at the straw market, and dining like royalty.

I felt so blessed to have a sister like her to share a day like this. She had no idea that day how she helped me take another step in life.

She held my hand and gave me the courage to step aboard another ship. When 2 1/2 years ago I vowed never to step foot on one again.

After a plentiful day, I asked Debby to share with me a little memorial to James. I wanted to take the carnations that we received today from boarding and give them up to the sea for James.

She wholeheartedly agreed. So that night we went to the back of the ship and leaned up against the rails. We spoke to James in the stillness of the night with all the twinkling stars around us.

There was not a sound except the crashing of the waves against the ship. I then out loud said "Because of your love of the sea and ships, I am here with you."

We kissed our carnations and threw them into the sea. Not a word was spoken and we both stood as if we were frozen in time.

I knew neither her thoughts nor she mine. But I am sure James was on her mind like he was mine. - How could this be?

We hugged each other and just stared out at the ocean. A treasure lost at sea.

Three years ago when our family was on our cruise we went to the isle of Roatan. It had mountains and little villages that seemed tribal and remote.

James and I stood at the rails and he asked me "Mom? Do you think pirates came here?" "Yes" I replied. "Do you think there's buried treasure?" "Of course," I said.

Looking back with sadness in my heart I remembered that conversation at the rail. Who would say? Who would know that ten months later, I had to bury my treasure?

The Death of Anna Nicole

Anna Nicole died last week
I knew her pain
No one can convince me
That she died of anything else but a broken heart.

6 Feet Tall

It was a Sunday and I was at church. As usual, I found myself chatting with friends.

I walked over to the coffee bar where I was greeted by a tall young man.

"Good morning Mrs. Everett." "Good morning," I replied, very startled.

He looked familiar but I couldn't quite place his face. "It's me, Tyler." he exclaimed.

"Tyler?!"

To my shock it was one of James' friends. I couldn't believe it!

He had grown so much and his facial features had changed.

Not to mention, he was also 6 feet tall!

Wow, for a second I felt betrayed. He had changed, he was growing up.

Up until this moment James was frozen in time. He was still 13.

I pictured him the same height, long blonde hair and lanky build.

But Tyler was his buddy and he was 15.

James did not see 15. James did not have the chance to grow up.

For a second I imagined him tall and thought, by now he would have been six feet tall!

The wave of tears like a tsunami came over me, without warning and uncontrollably.

I broke down and cried.

My friend Sue Grajko rushed me to another room.

There I cried bitterly and said over and over "He would've been six feet tall by now."

I imagined how handsome he would have been and

How his facial features would have matured.

In my mind he was beautiful. Yet, I wept bitterly for he was not here!

I have neither the privilege nor the pleasure of watching him grow.

Oh Lord give me the strength, when I see another child grow;

Make me strong and help me just to remember my own.

February 20, 2006

Today is a holy day for me. It anniversary of the day James was born. I remember being told by the doctors that he may not survive birth. Yet by Gods miraculous hand he lived but only till thirteen.

Thirteen wonderful years. Pure joy and sunshine did he bring to our hearts, pure love was what he demonstrated to us. Happy birthday James, today you are sixteen.

I am sad that I cannot see you. I am sad that I cannot hug you. Today I was only able to touch the cold marble with your name inscribed.

Instead of gathering around the table with cake and ice cream, singing and laughing, the family gathered around your grave and wept bitterly. I do not think of you as a year older but just another year without you.

How much things have changed! How much our love for you has been! My prize, my treasure, my sweet little baby boy. Happy birthday, James.

You were a pleasure to be around and truly a gift from heaven for us all.

A Cry for Help

This is an e-mail that I wrote to send out to all my friends, but never did.

Hello everyone.

This is Monica.

I am writing this because it is impossible
To call everyone and it exhausts me.
James' birthday is coming up on the 20th.
I desire to be normal and have a party with his friends,
But he is not here.

I have been hurting so bad. I miss James. I miss Joey.
My life is so different now. It hurts just to breathe...
I have not been functioning at work so well this week...
My family is broken. We are incomplete.

I miss our family nights.
I miss kissing my kids goodnight, especially since the absence of James.
I've been so sad!
The frustrating part is that there are no answers!
.
I feel like an alien... everyone around me is still the same and with their family,

It's hard to watch them. Will you please send me a kind word?
I am hurting so bad.

Is anybody out there?????

The Glimpse

I caught a glimpse of you today, James.

I was traveling from Miami to Newark, New Jersey. A tall blonde
boy with long hair came on board.

His eyes were blue and his skin tan and smooth.

His family came back from a cruise. He was probably about six feet
tall just like I would have imagined you.

He had that similar shy smile and that tilt of the head when he said
hello to me. Once we were airborne shortly after then I began
our service.

I froze when I came to his row. He had fallen asleep and looked like
an angel. Wow I thought, it is not James but just a glimpse of
James.

I took a deep sigh and found myself lost in thought. I wanted my
eyes to be transfixed upon him and to think that it was James.
But I knew it was not him.

His blonde hair covered his face and his features were similar.

In my heart I said, thanks Lord; thanks for the glimpse. Thank you
Lord for letting me see him in human form.

I quickly then returned to my service. I walked up and down the
aisle as my duty,

But always stopping by his row to catch a glimpse of James.

4:50 pm 2/24/07

Torment

March comes in like a lion so they say, and how true it is!

I sat on the tarmac waiting to deplane. We had a terrible storm and the flights have all been delayed.

I struggle with my thoughts and I feel I am exhausted. I fight all day to keep sane and to keep my tears from flowing;

To fight the emotions of anger, bitterness and guilt.

It was a long battle and now I am weary. It makes me weak. The days are long but the nights are torturous.

I cannot control my dreams or thoughts when I am asleep.

I am tormented day and night. I toss and turn all night with dreams of James or what could've been.

I am afraid to go to sleep this evening. I wonder what strange dreams will pop up tonight.

I give credit to parents who lost a child due to horrific events or those who are just plain missing.

How do they cope? Never knowing!? Or worse! Knowing that their child suffered in the hands of an evil person.

Lord I know my burden is much to bear, but Lord be with those parents whose burden is even greater. Comfort them. Comfort the broken mother. Comfort the broken father.

And bring those missing children home. Amen

11:20 pm
3/1/07

Lamentations

Day and night I lament for thee,
Day and night I think of thee.
Is there no end, is there no peace?
What will then become of me?
Oh James, can't you see
That my heart bleeds for thee?

11:45 pm
3/11/07
EWR to ATL taxi

MY heart and soul bleed for thee.
MY heart and soul long for thee.
Where is the other side of me??

Why did you go?
Don't you know?
You were everything to me?

The sea was quiet today.
It was still as glass,
As if it had no reason to play.
I stared at the sea and it stared
Right back at me.
The sea seemed nothing without James there to play,
It was as if the sea were sad to see,
That I was without thee.

YOUR NAME I LONG TO SAY ALOUD
Your name hangs on my lips;
I want to speak your name,
I want to call out,

So you will come.
But silence is all that speaks to me........

My spirit seemed to have left me that dreadful day.
I died, then I fell to the ground.
I turned cold when I entered the morgue;
I too was buried spiritually when
His casket was entombed.
My soul felt pain then left me hollow.
WHAT?
WHEN?
HOW?
THAT DAY MY BABY BOY HAD DIED...

Did you ever feel such pain?
Did you ever feel such loss?
Not in all my years of life have I ever faced such a loss.

Do you wish to die?
"NO", I SAID.
Do you wish to live?
"YES", I SAID.
"For my family."

I LOVE MY BOYS!
I LOVE MY HUSBAND!
They are everything to me!!
The only things that matter to me,
Are Brooks, Ricky and Joey.

"Who loves you more than life itself?"
I used to ask my James!
"You do!!!" He would reply.
Oh yes, I did.
I almost died, because of my love for you.

Was it not evident?
Was it not understood?
I did love him more than life itself!!
I told him he was the sun, the moon and the stars to me!!!
Is it no wonder that I almost died?
Is it no wonder now that I barely live?
My mind is tormented day and night.
Without you by my side I feel I can no longer be alive.
WILL YOU HELP ME LORD?????
I have two boys that I dearly love, but my pain for James
Is still too great for me.
How can I breathe?
How can I live?
How do I go on?
Will you help me, Lord??

Spring

Spring is the beginning of new life.
Spring brings changes;
It brings the dead back to life.
Spring gives birth to butterflies and birds.
Springs air is crisp and clean.
Spring's fragrant dance delivers heavenly scents
For the goodness of our souls.
Spring makes us glad to be alive!
Spring.
You were spring.
You were a new beginning for me.
When I was tired or weary, you brought me back to life again,
Just with your enchanting smile.
Your voice was like the melody of the birds that sing in spring.
Your soft voice and gentle, caring, spirit was like the fragrance
    of flowers to my soul.
You made me glad to be alive.
I remember saying to myself, one day,
"I look forward to the rest of my life with this child."

SPRING! Yes, you were spring
But you were only here till spring.
For that was your last season with us.

Just Like Spring

Today I went to the store and bought some flowers.
I then proceeded to the crash site.
I began to arrange them around the cross. I picked out spring
flowers for you:
The daffodils, wisteria, poppies, and forsythia.
While I was arranging them I began to think how you were like the
spring.-
Except you were year round.
You always had that amazing spirit that would light up the room
when you walked in. Your smile was like sunshine and your eyes
were like dew drops glistening in the sun. When you spoke it was
enlightening and enchanting.
For your soul was like the peaceful feeling of a quiet spring morn.
Such peace,
Such tranquility,
Such purity, incredible joy.
Like spring, your beauty was young and fresh.
Just like the flowers that bloom in the spring, they are here for
awhile and then are gone.
Just like you James, in the seasons of life, you were spring.
Your spirit, your heart and your life!!
Now you are gone and only winter is left.
At least, that is how it feels.
Oh how I wish, spring was here and I could feel alive and new
again!!!!

Too Short

EVERYTHING ABOUT SPRING WAS YOU.
LIKE SPRING,

YOUR LIFE WAS TOO SHORT.

5, Then 4

All the while the children were growing; I delighted in finding
characters or symbols of 3 and 5. Whenever I saw 3 little pumpkins
or 3 little puppies together, I would say, "That's just like my 3 little
boys!" If I found things in 5, I was lucky! For that represented my
family. I was shopping one day and came across 5 little birds on
a small planter. They appeared to be conversing with each other. I
immediately bought it and placed it in the garden.

I found it the other day, empty with weeds in its place and thought,
There they are, all happy as can be, still singing and conversing, a
gentle reminder of how we use to be...

There we were as happy as could be

All five of us together

Living, loving and laughing

Till one tragic day

One of us was taken away.

No longer is it 5 but 4

Our laughter turned to tears.

And now the only symbol that remains.

Is a ceramic reminder of how we use to be.

Anna Nicole

Anna Nicole
Was laid to rest, next to her son,
Was her request.
She was adorned with satin, tulle and pink.
A sparkly tiara was placed upon her head.
A large pink flowered heart draped over her chest.
A symbol to all that she died of a broken heart.
It's the saddest death I know!
A broken heart,
Over the loss of a son.
I too know this loss.
So go Anna Nicole, and be with your son.
Together you should be.
TOGETHER was the only road you knew,
TOGETHER are you now both, for eternity.

Does Five Years Matter?

I went back to work today.
It is my second attempt.
Another attempt to enter the land of the living.
It takes so much of my energy to be strong; to push back the tears;
To listen without judgment.
To people who whine and complain about simple things
That aren't broken or lost.
About trivial things that can be resolved.
Think about it:
*Most everything in life has a solution.
*Solve and make steps toward that solution.
*Loss of job? You can find another.
*Loss of home or car?
*You can attain another.
*Loss of son?
FIN!
I was angry at my friend once when she complained about her son
Who was in the hospital, not responding as quickly as she hoped.
I thought to myself, "She has something to work with, something
to hope for."
In 5 years her son has a chance of being well. I do not have that
hope.
Five years from now my son will still be gone.
He does not have a chance of getting better.
5 or 10 years will be a big improvement for their son, but not mine.
He will still be gone. I do not have any one to work with.

Vines

My husband is a wise man. His faith is strong.
He has endured incredible loss and yet he still stands.
I, on the other hand, have not been strong, especially regarding the
death of our son.
I told my husband that we needed to talk.
He replied with, "Let's walk around the property."
We strolled around the yard and I went on and on about my
difficulties:
My sister, her kids and my father who all just moved in with us,
My health, and my job.
It seemed overwhelming for me even as I spoke about it.
We had finally come full circle and he stopped in front of a tree.
My husband told me to look at this tree.
The tree was tall but had been broken in half. It was a ghastly site!
Wisteria & muscadine vines had entangled it so much that the tree
could not get enough Sun, therefore it could not grow or heal.
My husband then began to say, "Your life is like this tree right now
and the vines are like the struggles and worries that entangle you.
The tree is broken, just like you.
The tree cannot grow or mend because of the vines.
They are choking it.
You need to cut the vines and free the tree."
Working out in the yard so much I knew exactly what he meant.
"Lord, please help me with my vines so that I can be free, once
more."

YOU'VE GOT MAIL - A LAMENT

AFTER WATCHING "YOU'VE GOT MAIL" WITH MEG RYAN
& TOM HANKS
THIS LINE JUMPED OUT AT ME AND I WROTE IT DOWN
BECAUSE IT WAS SO SIGNIFICANT.
EVEN WHEN JAMES DIED, MY MOTHER'S DEATH CAME
BACK TO ME CLEAR AS DAY.

"I MISS MY MOTHER SO MUCH SOMETIMES I CAN
BARELY BREATHE.
I FEEL A PART OF ME DIED,
AND MY MOTHER DIED ALL OVER AGAIN,
AND NO ONE CAN EVER MAKE IT RIGHT."

THAT'S HOW I FELT WHEN JAMES DIED
I FELT LIKE MY MOTHER DIED AGAIN

A Tiara for My Mother

I heard when they buried Anna Nicole they placed a tiara upon her
head.
I found that gesture moving & significant.
I thought about my mother.
Of course, I was so stricken with grief- I couldn't think straight!
As I looked back, I wished I could have done that for her.
A tiara for my mother because
She was a princess; a CHILD OF THE KING.
And she has entered into his kingdom.
I wish I could have placed that tiara on her head when we put her
to rest.
I sometimes wonder and I'd like to think
That when she entered heaven, Jesus placed a real crown on her
head.

Angel in the Sky

I Flew from L.A. to Cleveland with a flight attendant I got to know well. She was a delightful lady and sweet as pie. I find it comforting to know that on my journey through the valley God places helpful people in my path.

I know these people come from Him. This woman is a devout catholic, married, but never had children. I think she would've made a great and wonderful mother.

She had so much love. We began our work and of course the age old question of "How many children do you have?" prompted my story.

That day was definitely a divine day for me. I know she was not just an ordinary woman but a woman God used to lift and inspire me. She went on to explain how her best friend lost a child 8 months after it was born, then lost a 22 year old in a tragic accident. Her middle son too, was in an accident and became a paraplegic. She then went on and explained, "I do not know your pain but I have walked with pain and carried her suffering through her tragedies."

I did not refute her statement. I asked how that mother could be alive. She then mentioned that it was her faith, her friends and her family, to which I nodded in agreement.

That too, is how I am alive. This woman was an inspiration to me because she was so encouraging. It is difficult for me to process everything or even write down everything because her words were so healing. For a second there, I felt like we were all alone and I had forgotten we were on the airplane.

There was a strange aura in the galley and she began saying how proud James was of me and what a fabulous example I had been to others.

My love and passion for him and my sons was so obvious. She spoke very softly but repeated over and over, "You are a good mother and your family seems to be a strong unit. James is proud of you."

It seemed like an out of body experience. It seemed as though the whole world faded away. As she spoke it was enchanting. It seemed like forever when we were interrupted by another flight attendant.

She had pulled me in so much that I nearly had to shake my head to snap out of it. What an incredible moment it was. For the rest of the day I was walking in the clouds.

Even way after the plane landed, her encouraging words lifted me to great heights. Another conversation we engaged in was about my house. She told me about a book called The Widow of the South. It was about a woman who lost her husband during the Civil War.

She opened up her plantation home to be used as a hospital. She took care of the boys and nursed most back to health. For those who died; she buried them in her backyard.

No one claimed their bodies, so she took it upon herself to tend and take care of their graves. Long after the Civil War ended, families would come around and look for their long lost boys.

She would try to help by sharing photographs and personal belongings she kept along with their names. Many were claimed and re-interred in their family plots.

Others were never claimed. But she tended to them as if they were her own. She adorned them with flowers and put out flags.

"An enlightening story", I thought. We then began to share stories of the south and history. It was a delightful day and an enchanting one as well.

It was a shame to see it come to an end. After she left I thought about how much she counseled me. How she made me aware of issues I was dealing with.

I had four and half hours with her and it felt like an incredible counseling session except it was with a good friend. Again it reminded me of God's hand in my life and how he cares for me.

She and I even spoke about the fact that we met. Sixteen thousand flight attendants, two different religions and yet we ended up on the same flight.

She said, "It was no coincidence. It had to be a higher power at work."

I definitely agreed.

He Was There

Can one see death and live?

Can one see hope after death?

Not at first,

But then you see

God's compassionate presence.

Then you will feel and see

He was there...

Even when I thought I was abandoned.

He was there...

Even when I thought I was betrayed.

He was there...

When I questioned His work and turned my face against the Lord.

He was there...

When I lay in that hospital bed, trying to catch a breath.

He was there...

When I thought I was going mad.

He was there...

When in the still of darkness I cried.

He was there…

When I screamed and cried…all through the night.

He was there…

Because He heard my cries and screams.

He was there…

Because He sent special people my way.

He was there…

Because He provided for my needs.

He was there…

Because he dried my tears.

He was there…

Because He restored my faith.

He was there…

Because He sent me angels of mercy disguised as friends

He was there…

Because He placed me in a sanctuary.

He was there…

Because of Him I am alive.

I survived the death of my son.

He was there…

Because He loved me.

Not Today

We were vacationing in Siesta Key for the week and to our dismay, it was the week of Red Tide – a natural phenomenon that produces excess algae in the Gulf of Mexico and kills marine life. It was a shame to walk the beaches and see hundreds of dead fish washed upon the shore.

Fortunately, after three days, the red tide passed and the beach began to clear up. I was wading in the water one early morn when I noticed a brown object in the water. At first I thought that it might have been a shell, but when I went to pick it up, it moved. It was a fish, and it was dying. It was a beautiful fish with streaks of all shades of browns and oranges. I thought to myself, "Poor fish, it looks like me: practically motionless on the ocean floor of life." Obviously the bacteria got him and he would die shortly. The death of James is my ailment and I am sure that someday it will take me. Never underestimate the power of a broken heart or a broken spirit. It is a daily battle just to make it through another day.

I was somehow mesmerized by this fish who obviously was struggling to stay alive. The waves broke and pushed him closer to the shore. With each wave, the motionless fish would perk up and try to swim against the tide even though he was on his side. Each wave crashed and pounded him closer to the shore. And each time, although on his side, he continued to fight with all that he had left, using only his wearied tail. At one time a wave washed him on shore, but then another wave brought him back to the sea. I was so impressed with this fish that was so determined to live. I thought for sure he would wash up and die, maybe, just like me: but he didn't – he continued to swim. I followed him until he swam into deeper waters and I could follow him no more.

I was proud of that little fish. He put up a good fight all while he was diseased and on his side. I knew that he would eventually die; it would only be a matter of time. I am sure that he knew it as well, but he was determined he would not die today. Watching the struggle of that fish made me think of my own struggle in the sea of life: broken, weak, and the battles of life pushing me closer to the end. I thought, after that lesson that surely the death of James will eventually take my life for no one knows the depth of love that I have for that child. But like the fish, I decided, "not today."

PROFOUND LIVING

I LIVE DEEP;

I LOVE DEEP;

I GIVE DEEP.

I APPRECIATE EACH SOUL THAT COMES MY WAY

AND TAKES THE TIME TO CARE.

I APPRECIATE THE SOUL WHO GIVES HIS PRECIOUS
GIFT OF TIME.

I CANNOT BEAR ANYONE'S CRIES;

FOR I KNOW IT INVOLVES PAIN.

I EMBRACE THE ONE WHO CRIES

AND TRY TO COMFORT THEIR BROKEN HEART.

MAYBE BECAUSE I WISH SOMEONE COULD HELP
ME

STOP CRYING FROM WITHIN.

IF YOU DO NOT SEE TEARS ON MY FACE

IT IS BECAUSE THEY HAVE DRIED UP.

BUT MY CRIES ARE STILL THERE.

THEY NEVER STOP.

BECAUSE THEY COME FROM THE DEPTHS OF MY SOUL.

SO, I WILL HELP STOP SOMEONE ELSE'S TEARS;

SOMEONE ELSE'S PAIN.

BECAUSE THEN,

AT LEAST,

I CAN HEAR THAT THEIR CRIES HAVE CEASED.

PROFOUND LIVING

LIVING, LOVING AND GIVING TO THE WEAK AND BROKEN HEARTED.

LIVING FOR OTHERS

LIVING FOR JESUS

Visiting With My Son

On a flight once, while we were in our jumpseats, I was looking out the window of the plane. The other flight attendant called my name several times. I did not hear her. When she finally got my attention, I apologized for not hearing her earlier. She said, "That's alright. You were visiting with your son, weren't you?"

"Where were you?" she asked.
"Visiting with my son," I replied.
"We were walking along the beach, picking up seashells"
"I was watching his blonde hair blowing in the wind."

Though at times I may appear aloof or distant,
Do not take offense,
For I may be visiting with my son.

A Mother's Sorrow

I am so sad, it's almost scary. There seems to be no joy. I have been
robbed of joy.
I need to look forward to something and I just can't seem to find it.
My family is my joy and Lord knows how I love those boys. But I
don't see them enough for they are older and on their own. I cannot
ask them to stay. I miss my three little boys. I miss being at home
with them.

Cries in the Seas

Poem 8/25/07

If you walk out by the sea and think you hear cries and moans,

Do not be afraid! For you are not mad! It is probably me!

I have been there, standing in the water,

Crying out to James.

My cries can still be heard as

They bounce off each and every wave.

Many tears were spilled there, but gently washed away.

James was that you??

Martha's Vineyard

How I miss you, James. I miss you so much. I went to Martha's Vineyard and thought about you constantly. I would have loved to have been wealthy and live on that island – so carefree.

There were so many places to explore. I know you would have loved climbing the rocks, running out to the cliffs and visiting the light houses. I imagined you running barefoot, your hair blowing in the wind with the backdrop of the ocean waves crashing onto the rocks. How wonderful that vision was; how beautiful you looked in my memory.

I went to Martha's Vineyard for inspiration and that was exactly what I received. I was hoping to get garden ideas and to see beauty in a new place. What I didn't expect, was to find you – to catch another glimpse of you.

I was standing out by the lighthouse point where the rocks stood high above the ocean. The sun was setting and the view was magnificent. No day could have been more perfect. I thought about life, I thought about you, and I wished that things could have been different. It was then that my friend, Lynn, called me to look at something. I started down the trail to hear an over-excited friend exclaim, "Monica, hurry! Monica, look!" Down below, in the grassy field, was a tall young boy, probably twelve or thirteen, holding a soccer ball.

His long blonde hair seemed to be everywhere. His lanky build was similar to James'. We were stopped in our tracks with our mouths opened in disbelief. All we could do was watch; watch this boy who reminded us so much of James. He and his buddies ran onto the field to kick the soccer ball around. I watched him dart in and out just like I used to watch James. Seeing him move around the field, laughing and having such a good time, it was as if I drifted into a dream, and I was once again, watching James play soccer with his buddies. Only this time, there were rolling hills on one side and the ocean on the other. What a beautiful vision that was; something that I will keep forever in my mind and in my heart.

Thank you, Lord. I know that it was not him, but you gave me another glimpse of him. We watched in awe, this boy playing soccer in the field, and for that memory, I am eternally grateful.

Newport

On this trip I visited Newport, Rhode Island. I did not expect to have the surprise and the awe that awaited me. It was another beautiful day with not a cloud in the sky. (Sunshine, 70 Degrees) No day could have been more perfect. Little did I know the beauty that I was about to see. We took an hour ferry ride over to Newport. Upon our arrival we were delighted to see the port with its colorful row boats, sail boats and docks just like you've seen in pictures & movies. The captain was familiar with Newport and took us all sightseeing down cobble stone streets, old colonial settlements and turn of the century graveyards. He then proceeded to take us down mansion row. We could not get over the size and opulence of these homes. Tall black iron gates adorned with gold leaves, immaculate gardens with statues, stained glass windows and architecture that I have only seen in my travels to Europe. One was better than the next. I felt transformed. Our captain then told us we were gong to take a hike. It was the "Cliff Walk" of Rhode Island.

What I was about to see, did not prepare me for the impact it was going to have. I was literally speechless. The Trail was high above the sea along the rocky cliff of the Island. On one side we heard the sea crashing on the rocks and the other sides were enormous grand mansions & castles. As we hiked along this trail, I was awestruck by the beauty of the ocean and the natural formations of the rocks. The sound of crashing waves upon the rocks and how water shot out of air pockets and crevices was astounding. One could stand there all day and not know how much time had passed, nor cared. There are roses that grow wild there, and all along the edge you will find green tall grass growing, honeysuckle vines and the sweet smell of crisp clean air. The air was so pure. I now know what clean air smells like. I just had to stop several times and take a deep breath. It was as if I was breathing in new life each and every time.

We hiked about 10 miles that day. I could not get over the size of each mansion and of course, each with immaculate gardens. All of them boasted Grand Ballrooms, tea rooms and servant quarters. Of course, I wished I lived there. As I hiked up and down each trail, stopping to look at the magnificent ocean & breathing new life, I thanked God for allowing me to have this wonderful moment. I know my eyes have seen great things and I am thankful. As we hiked, every corner revealed new beauty, more breathtaking than the next.

Then came that moment, that pinnacle, when we come around the peninsula. We were at the highest point. There were jagged cliffs with caves below and waves crashing among them. There, in that corner, stood a mansion. There were so many rooms and windows so that no matter what window you looked out, there was a view of the ocean. It was so stunning and spectacular that it stopped me in my tracks. My friend Lisa walked around and said, "So what do you think?" I couldn't say anything. I was left speechless. I tried to speak, but nothing came out. Just then, as I took in that wonder, a song began to play in my head. I did not look at that house and wish for it, but realized if man can do this, God can do better.

If this beauty and opulence I witnessed by man stunned me, then imagine what our heavenly Father has in store for us. I began to sing. *I've got a mansion just over the hilltop. In that bright land where we'll never grow old and someday yonder, we will never more wander but walk on streets that are the purest gold.* I was baffled by the size of this mansion that I beheld and thought of James, my son, living with God and living in a mansion. I was intrigued that when I looked back on the trail, each neighbor had a mansion and each one with its own unique architecture and style. Some were made of pure marble and some stone. But each one had its own style and character. You could almost guess what kind of person was living in each house by its style. No two were alike. As I looked back, I commented to my friend, "Imagine that, who could be jealous of their neighbor? Everyone has a mansion. Everyone has gardens and over 100 rooms."

That's when I caught just a glimpse of how it will be in heaven, each & every one of us living in our mansion. Each carefully designed to that individual by our Father's hand. I had a thought: a happy thought. JAMES! James being in a mansion designed especially for him. During my life with him, I wanted to give him the best. Now James has everything. Now James has a mansion and he holds the hand of Jesus!

A Painful Reminder

I had to tell your story again today.
I had someone intrigued with all the details. I went over all the
events that took place. Throughout the day we had a few breaks on
the plane to continue, but it exhausted me.
It made me sad.
At one point I had to stop because I remembered asking the Lord
to not take my baby from me. I stopped; I couldn't say anymore
because I remembered being in that office collapsing to the floor,
face down and begging God that it be not him.

I remembered the pain.
I remembered the surge of excruciating pain coming over me as I
entered "The Club".

New Life

This was written after my niece, Angelina was born.

Dear little Angelina Margarita,

Welcome to this world!

Welcome to our world!

You were born into a family who loves you.

You were born into a family who cares.

You bear the sweetest name of all:

Margarita.

She who bore the sweetest name

Our mother Margarita.

How sweet and precious is that name to us.

How sweet and precious is she

In our heart and in our memory

Carry your name with pride;

Shed not a tear;

For you are named after our queen

Who now resides in heaven.

From Here to There

It is early and I am on a working on a flight. The flight attendants I work with are great. We usually end up chatting and sharing life's ups and downs. In my situation, when they ask about family, I take a deep breathe and proudly bring up my boys yet carefully let them know that one is in heaven. This usually prompts heart to heart talks. The human spirit never seems to amaze me. No matter what that person's background is, people are touched by loss or sadness. They gather up their courage and help. I am a stranger to them, yet they embrace me and give me words of wisdom, council and encouragement. Many, many flight attendants that I have worked with have helped me take the next step. Many had the wisdom to see clearly and encourage me in so many ways. This was one of those times, thanks to this one particular flight attendant. She helped me make it to the next level.

After I explained my story, I plopped down on the jump seat exhausted, and said, "I can't believe I am still alive after all that has happened. That's just too much!"

My friend listened and replied with; "Sometimes we do not know why things happen to us but maybe it is because God wanted to take you to the next level."

With all the animation she possessed she drew an air graph and said, while pointing down, "You were here" then she pointed up and said, "But God wants you there."

To many, that may sound trite, but to me, because of where I was in my life, it made a lot of sense.

"Well" she continued, "sounds to me like, God has a purpose for your life. He may have a reason for you to be here. Maybe there is someone that is sick or is at the end of their rope, ready to do something drastic. You may be that person to stop them. You may be that person to make a difference."

Thank you, my friend in the sky, because of your insight, I will.

The Door to the Other Side

When you have stood at the door to the other side

You gain a new perspective.

You become the wiser.

No longer are you caught up with idealistic

Or fantasy dreams but the reality of your purpose on this earth.

Your vision becomes clearer.

Your every day decisions come out of the gray and into

The black and white.

How did this happen you say?

I was once close to heavens door.

Two precious people in my life walked me there...........

But left me standing in the cold. They went on and I

Was left behind. First was my Dear Mother. In her last days at hospice,

She would call out to her mother (who is also in heaven)

Every time she woke up and then end with

"COME BACK!!! COME BACK!!!!!!"

I would try to keep her comfortable and calm,

Always reassuring her that we were there for her. But every time she awoke,

She would call out to her mother again.

This went on for two days. On that

Second and last day, she woke up and

Reached towards the heavens and called out in her quaint British accent,

"MUMMY! COME BACK!!"

Again, I tried to hold her and tell her it was OK.

But her eyes moved passed me and she tilted her head to see above me

And called out again, "MUMMY!"

This time I could see in her eyes that she saw something!

I looked up towards the ceiling but there was nothing there.

Then I looked back at her. I saw the look on her face.

And I was startled, she saw something.

AS CHILLS WENT DOWN MY ARMS & SPINE I SAID,

"GO.........RUN!..... RUN MOMMY!..... GO TO HER! RUN TO HER!"

This scenario happened twice, then she went to be with the Lord

With her children all around her, and CHRIST AND HER
MOTHER WAITING

FOR HER AT HEAVEN'S DOOR.

MY MOTHER LEAD ME TO A PLACE WHERE I CAUGHT A
GLIMPSE OF

THE DOOR TO THE OTHER SIDE.

My life changed from there on out.

And that was only the beginning

"ENOUGH!" YOU SAY,

"HOW COULD THERE BE MORE??"

But yes, there was one more time when the one to lead me to the
other side

Was an unexpected one. It was a child. A beautiful child,

AND THAT CHILD WAS MINE.

A parent's worst nightmare! My son James led me to heavens door.

13 YEARS OLD and killed in a car crash.

My baby James. My little pumpkin pie! The one I told everyday
that

He was the sun, the moon and the stars to me.

I have seen the gates! I have been to the door again.

Just two days after the funeral, when my heart gave me a punch in
the chest.

When my life was fought for all night long in that emergency

Room in our little town in Georgia.

But it didn't stop there.

It happened again around the anniversary of his death the next year
and

Then again on the first week of school.

How odd life is.

How sad life is.

How strange the heart is.

It gives you life and it gives you death.

I have seen real life and have tasted the bitterness of death.

But the death of my son was far more cruel and de-habilitating
than any other

Loss I have ever encountered.

Reduced to a vegetable months later, having to learn to walk,

Talk and live all over again.

It was at least 8 months before I could get behind

The wheel of a car and drive again.

Only a mother would understand this kind of pain.

This time I was at the door and knocking pretty hard.

But it did not open for me, no matter how much I wished it.

My son was on the other side.

But he was safe with Jesus.

He was with my mother.

He was with grandma and grandpa.

He was with the children of God.

His body was whole and he is a pure, sinless being.

His hair is gold and his eyes are now made with sparkle and
brightness

Of all the twinkling stars. He walks hand in hand with Jesus

And escapes only to be with my mother.

His bedtime stories are told by Moses and Abraham.

He is intrigued and enchanted all the day long. I can picture this,
James.

At times I imagine he dances with David.

I also imagine that he plays his drum, for the children of God.

They dance, sing and praise the Lord together.

My mother watches in pure happiness.

I've been knocking on heaven's door, but I could not come in. Someday I will, to walk hand in hand and catch up on all that we missed.

I am glad that your daddy was with you that day. He held you and had to hand you over to the arms of Jesus.

His voice fading out as Christ's became clearer. He did not see heaven's door, because he was kneeling at heaven's door, holding you.

We all had to leave you then. Only knowing you were in a better place.

Yes, my life changed again and my life was never the same again.

My vision became clear and I received a new heart.

I had to learn all over again how to walk, how to talk, and how to live.

Everything grey in my life has become black and white. Every decision that needed to be made has been made with great clarity and wisdom.

I now live and work with purpose and with a deeper dedication and passion towards the ones I love.

With heaven and Christ becoming more real than I could have ever imagined.

It Didn't Hurt

This was written for me by my husband.

Remember when I was a child and I would fall down? You would make such a big deal until I said, "It didn't hurt." Of course, you didn't believe me, but it was true. You always cared more about me than you did about yourself. Thank you.

On July 17, 2004 I went to see Jesus. And guess what – It didn't hurt. I'm OK, now. Nobody can hurt me. I don't fall, anymore. You don't need to worry about me, it didn't hurt.

I know that you miss me and that you hurt. I'm sorry about that, but please don't worry about me; it didn't hurt.

You always took care of me, but now Jesus does. He takes good care of me, too. I love you, I miss you, and I can't wait to see you, again. Because you love me so much, mom, I just gotta tell you one more time. It didn't hurt.

The Mighty Warriors

There are very few that have walked where I have walked.

The Valley of the shadow of death.

It is a dark place full of obstacles so jagged and deadly

That not walked correctly could be certain death.

The place is dark. There is no concept of time, day, or night.

There is no direction, no sign, of where to go nor how to survive it.

The air is filled heavy with sadness; moans can be heard from afar...

Strange chanting can be heard in the distance, but I could not make out

Any clear words.

Grief weighed on me heavily that it tired me so. The sadness,

If not careful will b r e a k   y o u r   h e a r t.

As it did mine.

The heaviness of the air and the grief I felt made it difficult to breathe.

I had to struggle and fight for every breath.

There were unseen arrows that seem to come out of nowhere.

They pierced my heart and my body. I ached everywhere, and thought I was bleeding.

But I looked and saw no wound; I touched and felt no blood.

But I knew that something had to be there because

Of the internal excruciating pain I felt.

There was neither relief nor remedy I could find to ease this pain.

My vision became impaired and confusion set in.

There seemed to be no rhyme or reason to what I said or did.

I came to the conclusion that I had gone mad.

I longed for an explanation or answer;

But I did not hear any words that could ever make this right.

As I stumbled to the ground, weary and tired

I craved nourishment.

My mouth parched, I longed for water, but everywhere I felt was dry.

I hungered; but what ever was in front of me

Crumbled and tasted bitter and sour.

Hungry and tired, I collapse to the ground.

I awoke because of the strange chanting I heard

And stumbled to get on my feet again.

All I could do was stand still, because I was afraid

I was afraid of the dark.

I was afraid to take a step knowing I could fall again.

I could not see the road ahead of me and I remembered what was behind me.

The Great Fall.

I became increasingly paranoid and frightened.

So I stood still, not moving, not thinking.

Time passes by or does it?

How long have I been here? Hours? Days? Weeks?

Now I do not hunger nor do I thirst.

I do not know the hour or day

I begin to panic because I can't breathe

So I struggle to concentrate. I tell myself;

Breathe; you must breathe.

And with all the power in my might;

I did it. I took one more breath.

I still feel strange though, dizzy, wired, yet exhausted.

I come to and I do not know if I was wide awake or asleep.

Why am I here?

Why can't I see?

Where's my family?

I have not been able to speak up until now, but when I do, it was the
name,

The name of the one I lost. Then everything inside of me

Strengthened just to be able to say his name...

James!

Then I remember the fall, I remember death.

I realize that I am in the valley I heard of as a child.

My memory quickly returns to James, his beautiful face

Again, I realize that I am in the shadows.

This time I collapse because I can not take it anymore.

Tired, hungry, broken and weak,

I fall, I weep, I sleep.

I wished never to wake up again, but I do.

I did because out of my sleep, I heard something very familiar.
Noise!

Conversation! Cries, pleas and prayers.

I heard the prayers and the voices of family, voices of friends.

Some, I haven't heard of in a long, long time.

Some, who I thought had forgotten me.

It gave me strength.

I lifted my head just high enough in attempt to contemplate the direction of the voices.

That's when I caught a glimpse of something shiny.

It was faint, but it was there. Starting to feel dizzy again, I lay my head down and sleep.

This time I awoke because I felt something. It was not an arrow or shooting pain

But a strong hand. He caressed my head and then I felt his two strong arms pick me up.

I could not see him but I could feel him. As he lifted me I sensed his strength.

My body rested upon his breastplate. I could hear the clanking of armor.

It must be a warrior, I thought to myself. And I can hear that there are many of them.

They gave me food and drink. They cleaned my scrapes and brushed my hair.

Then, they lifted me once more and began to walk.

The journey was difficult, with steep crevices and rocks.

It was rainy and cold and there were areas where I

Was sure they would loose their footing and drop me. But they never did.

When one got tired, another warrior would carry me,

The journey I could tell was rough for them; I could hear them struggle as they tried to climb.

I heard some weep but others would pray. All the while through this journey, they

had to endure my cries, moans and screams.

They continued with their payers.

I do not remember how long the journey had been.

I just seem to drift in and out and felt as if I were in a dream.

The continuous sound of clanking armor let me know that they were there.

After awhile, the journey seemed to take another turn, this time it was a valley without steep cliffs and terrains.

I began to come to because I heard singing. I heard the prayers. This went on for months.

One day I awoke because something was touching my cheek and it was warm.

I opened my eyes and had to close them again because of its brightness. It was the sun...

I could see the sun and I was aware that I was out of the dark valley.

I noticed how green everything seemed to be and I heard birds sing.

I looked in the face of my warrior who carried me to thank him and saw the face of my husband.

I turned around to look at this mighty army to find my family and friends walking behind me.

Where are your breastplates?? Where is your armor??

I am certain I heard it in the valley!!!!

My husband replied, I do not have a breastplate....and what warriors??

The warriors that carried me through the valley of the shadow of death! I shouted.

Only to realize at that moment, the warriors that carried me through the valley of death were my family and friends.

IN the darkness the Lord transformed them to warriors of light and gave them heavenly strength.

You were the mighty warriors!!! Strong; equipped with the armor.

Carrying the shield and breastplate of the Lord! You came in the name of the Lord!!

The chanting I heard in the valley were prayers, the moans in the distant was the singing.

You see, your acts of kindness

the help that you given to me and my family are greatly appreciated.

To me they are a gift from God. You may think your small act of
kindness may be insignificant

but while I was in the valley,

It brought water to my lips, food to my table.

A strong shoulder to cry on,

Strong arms to carry me when I could not walk.

Even if all you could do was pray, you kept me alive!!!

You were the one who helped me take that one more breath!

Some of you cried out in anger to the Father! You pleaded with
him!

You called upon his power to heal this broken heart.

I needed your prayers because I turned my face from God because
of my anger.

I loved my boy. I was angry that the Lord had taken him.

Your prayers brought back my heart from that hospital room

shortly after his funeral.

Your prayers saved my life and allowed me to see

His mighty work and the mighty love of his people.

I stand before you here today to thank you;

You, the mighty warriors who carried me through the Valley of the
shadow of death.

From Doubt to Faith

I am not better but the Lord has shown me that He is there. He has
bestowed several gifts to me. Every single one of you has been a
gift. Your phone calls, cards, emails and visits have made me see
God's love.
Never think of yourself trite or trivial when you commit an act of
kindness.
To me, it was a bag of gold. To me it was the difference between
my times of doubt and the road back to faith.

"O how marvelous, o how wonderful
Is my saviour's love for me."

Family Chain

Our family Chain is broken,
And nothing seems the same,
But as God calls us one by one,
The chain will link again.

The Gift of a Promise

My husband is a pastor on staff at Community Bible Church.
He sends out a Bible verse each day to anyone who would like to
    receive one.
He calls it the "Inverse". Naturally, one gets sent to our house.
This one ministered to me. It was sent out Dec. 05, 2006.
Jokingly I asked him if I could have that one on a plaque.
I need to see that as a daily reminder!
The following day was our anniversary. He had one made with a
    beautiful photo of the Colorado River and mountains in the
    background.
It was beautiful! That is my hope…a new heaven and a new earth.
The sound of weeping and crying will be heard in it no more.

Here is the verse:

"Behold, I will create new heavens and a new earth. The
former things will not be remembered, nor will they come to
mind. But be glad and rejoice forever in what I will create.
For I will create Jerusalem to be a delight and its people
a joy. I will rejoice over Jerusalem and take delight in my
people; the sound of weeping and of crying will be heard no
more."

Isaiah 65:17-19 (New International Version)

LETTERS TO MY SONS

I have enclosed a few letters that I had written to my surviving precious sons during this most difficult time in our lives. My life goal is to uphold and sustain their spirits. My love for my sons runs deep. Although I may not have all the answers to this life, I wanted to acknowledge their struggles and remind them of who they are and what they mean to my husband and me, for love is a powerful remedy.

UPON THE DEATH OF JAMES

My dearest Ricky,

I know you were there…
I know you saw the scene.
I know you were there to hold your Dad.

You are a wonderful son. A brave soul. I cried bitterly when I found out, you later arrived to the scene and saw what was going on. I never wanted you to have that kind of pain. I never wanted your eyes to behold such a sight! I heard you and Dad held each other crying. I heard you did not walk over to the wreck but stayed and held your Dad.

That dark and lonely evening, you were a soldier of light and comfort to your Father.

I AM SO PROUD OF YOU.

Mom

Ricky, my precious son,

I do not know what to say. What can I say? This should have never happened! Although James' death was tragic to me, the bigger tragedy was seeing your pain. I wanted to take it all away and I couldn't. I never wanted anything to hurt you. I was angry at everything because it hurt you, Joey and Dad. I am so sorry, my son, that your precious eyes had to see that. I wish it never happened. I love you and I know you are hurting, but remember this always: I will be here for you.

I love you, Mom

My dearest Joey,

I do not know where to begin, my sweet and beautiful son. All I know is just that I love you and want to do whatever I can for you. My heart breaks whenever I think of how hurt you have been. Sometimes I feel helpless and useless in comforting you. No one at your age should have to go through what you have gone through. I know that it has been tough. No, actually it has been like hell on earth. I so much want to take away all the pain and bring James back and make everything perfect for you. Trust me, if I could change it, I would. I know that you probably wonder why all this has even happened. Believe me, I do, too. This whole thing has been unbelievable. I am also at a loss as to what to do next. Where do we go from here? Well, I do know this: we are still the Everett family.

You have a mother and a father who love you dearly, and a brother who loves you and needs you. You have Aunts and Uncles in Clearwater, Fort Lauderdale, New Jersey, California, Ohio, and the list goes on. You have numerous friends scattered all over the USA which I might add, you can visit anytime because of my job perks. You have a God whom you may not understand, now, but we will when we get to heaven. Who knows? God may have spared James from a terrible future that he would have had to face. "The righteous perish, and no one ponders it in his heart; devout men are taken away, and no one understands that the righteous are taken away to be spared from evil." Isaiah 57:1

Interesting verse, isn't it? You know that I don't like trite answers, but this one makes sense to me. It is the only one. I hope that you can hold on to this verse like I can. I know it has been very hard. More than a person should have to bear. I know that sometimes the pain is so deep that you can't breathe. At times it hurts so much that I feel like someone is sitting on my chest. Please know and understand that we all feel that way sometimes. The other day, dad went to the crash site. He said that an overwhelming sadness came over him and he cried for an hour. Not just for me, but for you and Ricky, too.

You know that I might be a little over protective, but I am your mother and I care about you. I feel helpless sometimes. I just wish I could change everything and mend your broken heart. Please be patient with me. Please try to understand that I help because I care. I want you to know that I will always love you and I will always be there for you. Please know I will always have your best interest at heart. Family and friends may come and go, but a mother's love is always there, watching, waiting and willing to help.

Joey, you are my life,

Love, Mom

Peace

My dearest Ricky,

In this life there is hardship, but in the new life there will be true peace…peace of mind, tranquility and real love.

No one will hurt you and you will never shed a tear. My precious son, it is what we have to look forward to; heaven. For me it will be heaven, heaven with my boys. Knowing

That no one will ever hurt you and no one will ever be unkind, that is heaven to me!

I love you son, and if I could be in the forefront of all your pain and sadness, I would.

(I'm pretty shameful like that!)

Do not fear anything nor death when it comes. Remember son, you are a child of God;

A prince. You will rule in the next life right along with your brothers.

Hold your head high son; for you are a knight and a prince in my eyes and God's.

You are deeply loved and cherished daily.

With a love so deep and powerful that it would reach the farthest star, Mom

Imagine

My Dearest Joey,

I am so sorry to hear that some things did not work out the way you wanted. It was so hard to hear how upset you were. It broke my heart when you said that it was just another stone thrown on you. It felt like a boulder to me. How I wanted to hug you right then and there! Life is so hard son, I do know that. I wish I could have blocked those stones myself. Sometimes when things get so rough, I am speechless; I never know what to make of it! I never know what to say! I did learn this though over the years, and even more so with James.

We are here for only a while. It does not matter what happens here on earth. There is pain and there is suffering. Only in heaven will we be ok and safe. After James' death, all I ever think about is our reunion. When we will all be together and free from sickness, pain, injustice and suffering. God promised us a new kingdom and a new earth. We will live there for eternity. We will be together and living in a thriving community. Son, I know our family will be there and I have a notion that my sons and especially you, will be rulers of one of the kingdoms of heaven. You may have troubles here (as we all do) but in heaven you could be one of those elders that rule one of the kingdoms of heaven! Just imagine that!

Remember that here things may be a crazy, but you are a child of God which makes you a Prince! You are loved beyond measure by all of us. You, my son, will lead and rule in a peaceful kingdom. Imagine the look on James' face when he sees you coming. He will be there to meet you when it is your time to go. You will be embraced by our Lord and James will be there to give you his embrace. Imagine that joy on his face! "That's my brother!" is what he'll probably say. Imagine the pride on James' face as he stands next to you!

It is not about this life but the next. That is our hope. That is what we look forward to.

I know we will all be there together forever.

> With the greatest love and compassion one
> Could ever imagine, I give to you, Mom

Take It With You

My dearest Joey,

I am excited about your zest for life, your desire to learn and sense
of adventure. Can I blame you? For I too, have these same passions
for life. I enjoy my job. I have enjoyed my travels in the United
States and Europe.

When you told me about your new college experiences
and all the countries you wanted to visit,
I became scared.
I guess I am a little more afraid now because the world has
changed. It has become a more dangerous place. Yet fear shouldn't
stop us from living our life.
If you would just allow me to express a concern I have, I would be
happy if you would give this some thought.

Wherever you go, I want you to take a few things with you.

Your family name:
Never change it nor forget where you came from. Your roots are
important.
You have a father and mother who love and cherish you.

Remember the impact on us when we lost one of our boys.
We would have reacted the same way if it were you.
Our children are very precious to us.

Take with you your childhood memories of family trips to Disney
world, Montana
New York etc., birthday parties, family movie nights and playing
Ninja Turtles with your brothers.

Take with you the love of your grandparents on both sides who
loved and adored you. Remember the holidays, family reunions
and the fun you had.

Take with you the love of your brother Ricky, although growing up, brother's get on each other's nerve, remember his brokenness when he too, lost James and how he still struggles to this day..

Take with you the love and memory of your little brother James Michael.
Do not forget nor allow anyone to extinguish that light.
For in James death; he taught us many things and made us all the wiser.

We love life;
We value life;
We treasure our family;
We treasure our friends.
We know the value of spending time with someone we love.
We know to guard our lips from saying anything unkind or hurtful.
We know we have a good family.
We know we are the lucky ones.

Forget religion but remember your faith. Remember the truth in the Bible and the way to heaven.

Do not get caught up in philosophies or strange doctrines. Guard yourself, be careful.
As you know, life is short.
We will all meet our Maker someday regardless of our belief. It matters that you trusted Christ to get you to heaven.
Remember after all this is over my precious son,

We stand before God.

Not with religion, ideals or philosophies.

Just God and his Word.

We will all be reunited in heaven.
Nothing else matters.

So please be careful that no one sways you from the truth.
Look to the Bible for truth.
Do not let anyone try to confuse or change your true belief.

Remember your parents love for you.

Be careful when trying new "things."
Your body and health is all you have to keep you going.
You must save your body for what is yet to come.
Many people in your lifetime will depend on you.
It is important to be strong with a clear and sound mind.
Please do no harm to yourself for your family would suffer so
much,
As we have already been witnesses to.

We love you and care about you. We want the very best for you.
Please understand everything I say is because I do not want you to
suffer.
You can save yourself a lot of heartache down the road.

I am shocked to learn how many young people use some kind of
substance or aide
Just to get by. It saddens me.

Do not fall under pressure; just because they engage in a certain
activity does not make it ok.
Rise above it my son;
Be the one to stand firm and take care of your body and yourself.

There are many things in life that give natural pleasure and perks.
Find them. Seek out hobbies that will release natural endorphins to
make stress
Disappear and do them. Try sports; music; photography; or go to
the ocean,
Learn to sail.
I feel like these are obvious answers but really; give any of these
things a try. They work.

Everything I am writing to you please take to heart. Do not be offended or think I do not trust you.

I trust you, son.

Unfortunately in life, there are many people out there who do not have your best interest at heart.

Just please be aware of your surroundings and proceed with caution when you meet someone new.

Remember your family loves you.
Since you were little, you never needed anything to make you happy but sunshine itself.
I am delighted when I see your face light up over natural beauty and just life itself. It seemed as if you could not contain your excitement. I noticed it when we vacationed in Montana.
I remember when you were little and how excited you would get when you saw your friends.
Christmas, Disney world, puppies and toys; you loved them all.
Now I see you move onto bigger things:
You speak of history, discoveries, oceans and pyramids. Temples, far away lands and sailing the seven seas. That is you Joey. The world is your oyster

.

Just be careful. There are many traps, try not to fall into too many. Fall? Yes, for we are human and we all make mistakes.

You know the value of a life
You understand how everything we do affects so many around us.
James' taught us that too.

My precious son, Live, Love and Laugh;
But with a pure heart and a sound mind.

I love you.

Even if crazy things happen, and you come back to us and say;
"I've messed up my life! I hop on one foot and I can see out of
only one eye".
We will love you. We will care for you. You see, it doesn't matter.
Our love is unconditional. These are our wishes and guidelines for
your safety and well being.
You are my son. There is nothing you can do to make me stop
loving you. We will be here for anything and everything you need.
We will nourish and comfort you and help you get on your feet
again.
We will help you try to get on your feet again.
Many fall down by the minute, but the GREAT ones get up and try
again.
My dear son, we all have fallen sometime in our life but we get up.
You too must try.
Although I have just finished writing that sentence, I didn't need to
since I have
Already seen you go through many difficulties. You have already
overcome so much. I cannot begin to express how proud I am of
you. You have proven over
And over your loyalty to us and your maturity. A mother couldn't
be prouder.

I know many of these letters may not apply for right now but keep
them in your family box. Read them from time to time. Soon more
and more things will make more sense to you.

I love you my dear and precious Joey.
You are the world to me,

With so much love and admiration for you, Mom
XOXOOXOXOXOXOXXXOXOXOXOXOXOXOXOOXOXOXOX
OXOXOXOXOXOXOXOXOXOXOXOXOXOXOXOXOXOXOOXOX
OXOXOOXOXOXOXOOXOXOXOXOOXXOXOXOXOOXOX
OXOOXOXOOXOXOOXOXOOXOXOXOXOXOXOXOXOXXOX

CPSIA information can be obtained at www.ICGtesting.com
Printed in the USA
BVOW03s1613260713

326831BV00002B/678/A